# The Art of Gift Wrapping

Published in the United States by Potter Craft,
an imprint of the Crown Publishing Group,
a division of Random House, Inc., New York.
www.crownpublishing.com
www.pottercraft.com

**POTTER CRAFT** and colophon is a registered trademark of Random House, Inc.

Library of Congress Cataloging-in-Publication Data

Wen, Wanda.
**The Art of gift wrapping :**
50 innovative ideas using organic,
unique, and uncommon materials /
by Wanda Wen. — 1st ed.
p.   cm.
Includes index.
ISBN 978-0-307-40847-1
1.  Gift wrapping.   I.  Title.
TT870.W422 2010
745.54—dc22

2009014073

Printed in China

Design by **La Tricia Watford**
Photography by **Jules Bianchi**
Project Styling by **Vanessa Tamayo**

Special thanks to Sisters of Kent for allowing the use of magazine pages
featuring their graphics in the From the Glossies project, page 60.

10 9 8 7 6 5 4 3 2 1

**First Edition**

# The Art of Gift Wrapping

50 INNOVATIVE IDEAS USING ORGANIC, UNIQUE, AND UNCOMMON MATERIALS

WANDA WEN

POTTER
CRAFT

NEW YORK

# CONTENTS

# INTRODUCTION

*"It is better to give than to receive."*

We have all been there, circled around our friends and family, as package after package is held up, exclaimed upon, marveled over. Our emotions become heightened as the person receiving the gift takes a moment to reflect on her relationship with the gift-giver. And then the package is anxiously opened, revealing the precious gift inside. I love these fleeting moments.

I have always been conscious of the importance and value of making a good first impression, and for many years I worked in the fashion industry, where I was able to help people create unique looks for themselves. But at nights and on the weekends my true passion called to me—not fabric but paper. I squirreled away scraps and scrolls of paper I encountered in my daily life and in my travels. Soon I began sharing my favorite finds with others. Looped around envelopes, woven and wrapped around boxes, even sewn together into sheets, my paper collection became the highlight of each gift I gave.

In 1995, I decided to devote myself fully to my passion, and my West Hollywood paperie, Soolip, was born. Today my store has become a destination where individuals come to experience the so-called "Soolip Fix"— to be inspired and surrounded by those things most precious, those made by hand. Whether handmade cards, fresh flowers atop

beautiful gift wraps, calligraphic invitations, or home-crafted papers, the goal is the same: to live each day with beauty and inspiration. Not only is this the motto I've adopted for my business, it is how I approach my life.

But the joy in giving need not be dictated by fancy papers or elaborate ribbons. As you'll find in the pages that follow, beauty and inspiration can be found all around us, in everyday objects that most of us already own. In this book there is a wrap and a ribbon for every gift, from smooth river stones to the sparkle of gold leaf to the richness of velvet and jade. In the Organic & Natural chapter, I will show you how to mine your backyard for gift toppers that transform common findings in nature from simple to sublime. In the Resourceful & Inventive chapter, you'll learn how to use common household materials to wrap any present on a budget, creating modern, sophisticated looks that will be admired for their ingenuity. Turn to Eclectic & International for ways to pull together complete looks from any material—including those from around the globe. And for occasions when only the most sumptuous wrap will do, try the techniques shown in Lush & Romantic, guaranteed to dress your package to impress.

I believe that all of us have a gift-wrap artist within and that the possibilities for transforming a run-of-the-mill present into something truly spectacular are, indeed, endless. Use the unorthodox materials that I show you here as a springboard to create works of art for your loved ones. Most important, as you turn these pages, be inspired and have fun!

## DESIGN PRINCIPLES FOR INSPIRED STYLE

*With all the options in paper, ribbons, twines, accoutrements, gift toppers, nature's elements, and found objects, how do we begin to choose what to wrap with? The design principles that follow guide me every day in my work and life. These seven principles are evident in the examples shown here and in each wrap you'll find in this book—and can help you as you create new wraps of your own.*

1

3

2

01.

*"live each day with beauty and inspiration."*

4

5

6

## MIX HIGH AND LOW

You may be automatically programmed to pair formal paper with formal ribbon for chic occasions, and casual materials for more relaxed occasions. However, just as with fashion, mixing high-end and low-end materials is a treat for the eye, transforming a basic look into something special. For instance, the combination of an organic bark paper with a luscious hand-dyed silk ribbon can be appropriate for a formal setting, as well as a casual get-together. (It's also an example of design rule 6, Balance Textures, in action.) Or use a simply colored wax twine to pull out an accent color from a fancy Japanese yuzen paper (design rule 5). In both cases, the contrast between ornate luxury and bare-bones basics creates a push-pull dynamic—the upscale yin to the downtown yang.

Bundles of twigs look right at home on both fancy and casual wraps (photo 1). Use a luxurious material, such as the silk ribbon shown here, to go from down-home to upscale.

## 02.

### EMPHASIZE SIMPLICITY

Though we have grown accustomed to gifts sporting wide ribbons and bows, don't underestimate the sophistication of thin materials, such as twines, wires, yarns, and embroidery thread. Multiple wraps of a metallic-gold twine can create a deconstructed look. Secure a gift topper to the package and you'll have a modern approach to a dressed-up gift.

Long strands of narrow silk ribbon in a milk chocolate-brown, fuzzy yarn, and skinny gold twine meet in a square knot at the top of the package and are left to float freely, a simple embellishment that visually connects all the elements of this wrap (photo 2, page 9).

### BE PLAYFUL

Whether the gift you are wrapping is for a child's birthday or a sophisticated wedding, a feeling of playfulness and liveliness in the wrap will refresh and inspire, as well as bring an extra-wide smile to the recipient's face. In other words, listen to your creative instinct. If you are wrapping a gift for a friend's formal wedding, don't feel inhibited—go ahead and add that personalized gift topper, whether it's a dime-store reminder of a day at the beach, a cherished photograph, or a cup and saucer from the registry.

Soft white feathers stand out against the rough, rich Mexican amate paper, lending a fun, carefree spirit to this sumptuous package (photo 3, page 8). Though the techniques used here are simple, the look is anything but.

### BRING THE OUTSIDE IN

Each flower, each twig, each pebble, each piece of bark, and each seed pod is perfect just as Mother Nature created it. Take walks in your own backyard, in your local park, up mountain trails—wherever your feet lead you, you'll find unique elements of nature to dress up (or down) any package. Even a fallen branch of pods can make a perfectly interesting gift topper.

## 04.

Delicate peppercorn sprigs making a unique embellishment for this stack of packages (photo 4, page 9). Though the gold twine is merely wrapped multiple times around the stack of boxes, it's strong enough to hold the peppercorn sprigs in place. A metal florette finding anchors the twine, just an additional little detail sure to delight.

## 03.

## 05.

### ACCENT COLORS

When choosing colors to combine in a package, focus on your main wrapping paper. If using a patterned paper, highlight some of the less-prominent colors with ribbon. Or spice up a package with a ribbon in an entirely different, contrasting color. To learn which colors to combine and in which hues, tones, and saturation, you could spend years studying color theory. However, I think the best color primer can be freely found all around us. When choosing colors for a gift wrap, I often refer to the color palettes that nature has provided. Typically we think of earthy combinations of greens and browns or blues and greens. But don't forget about all the floral color combinations present in nature—the purple, green, and black passionflower; the white-and-yellow daisy; the pink and purple sweet peas; the vibrant orange, red, yellow and green field of poppies. Whatever gift you are wrapping, you are sure to be inspired by a brilliant color combination from nature.

Color and shine bring the elements of this wrap together. Glimpses of metal shimmer in the cork paper and are emphasized by the gold twine (photo 5, page 9). The carnelian-red velvet ribbon brings out the muted red in the screen-printed paper.

### BALANCE TEXTURES

Multiple textures can work together to create a sophisticated package. Try topping a finely textured fabric, such as gauze, with an object with a rougher texture, such as a twig, or overlay a smooth, solid Nepalese lokta with patterned lace paper. When layering textures on top of one another, try to keep a sensitive balance of light, medium, and heavy textures so the package looks substantial but not clunky.

A large piece of bark from a birch tree is unexpectedly layered between the two boxes, acting almost as a resting place for the package on top (photo 6, page 9). Both papers used here, a Mexican bark and a Lama Li fabric paper, are sturdy and highly textured to provide visual balance to the weight of the birch bark.

## 06.

## 07.

### LISTEN TO YOUR HEART

In the end, gift wrapping is all about creating a work of art with love to enhance the gift you are giving. So have confidence and delve into your own gift of creativity and choose materials that speak to you—whether through color, texture, or association.

*Look for Soolip Fixes throughout the book for extra insight on living each day with beauty and inspiration.*

# 01. GETTING STARTED

## Gift-Wrap Basics

*Over the years I have wrapped everything from tricycles to engagement rings, pomegranate trees to plane tickets. As wonderful as the gifts themselves are, I have always believed that each one is just a little bit better when dressed in a Japanese silk-screened paper or handmade lokta from Nepal, or finished with yards and yards of hand-dyed silk ribbon. But the first step to leaving a lasting impression is the most basic one.*

Choosing the right basic wrap for your gift will inform and inspire the paper, fabric, and notions that you use. Is your gift box a basic square or a flat rectangle? A round sphere or a tall cylinder? And how can you transform a simply wrapped present into a splendid, beribboned objet d'art?

Happily, the mastery of a few basic techniques and design principles opens the door to breathtaking wraps for any occasion—for birthdays, for holidays, or for no reason at all. As you proceed into the chapters that follow, you will discover that these basics are referred to time and time again, and that I build on them with other creative ideas. Give yourself the time and patience to learn these fundamental wraps and ribbon ties. Your packages will become more and more creatively inspired and take less time to create. You may find that the joy in wrapping for others becomes a joy in itself, and your thoughtful wraps will always leave a lasting impression.

## ALL ABOUT WRAPPING

TODAY, MORE THAN EVER, THERE ARE SO MANY OPTIONS OF PAPERS, RIBBONS, AND OTHER EMBELLISHMENTS TO CHOOSE FROM. IT IS CLEAR TO ME THAT WITH SO MANY CHOICES, DECIDING WHAT TO WRAP A GIFT IN CAN BE OVERWHELMING.

I approach gift wrapping with two things in mind—

**1.** that I am giving a little piece of myself, and
**2.** that I am honoring the gift recipient.

Thus, when choosing wrapping materials, I always choose elements that speak to me and reflect my style and character. I also consider the likes of the person who will be receiving the gift. For instance, if my gift recipient loves a specific color—say, purple—I would incorporate that color into the gift-wrap elements. If I know that my gift recipient is a nature lover, I will likely choose a plant fiber–based paper and affix a leaf or a bundle of twigs as a gift topper. If she is a sophisticated, fashion-conscious world traveler, I may opt for a more stylish luxe look of mottled gold paper layered over a rich chocolate-brown sheet. In essence, the aesthetic of a gift becomes a wonderful fusion of creativity, inspired by both my own style sense and that of the gift recipient.

Two other elements to consider are the occasion for which the gift will be given and the style of the place where the gift will be presented. As you would most likely put on elegant attire for an evening affair, and perhaps a casual, comfortable T-shirt for a picnic, there are times and places for dressed-up gifts just as there are times and places for dressed-down ones. You wouldn't wrap a present the same way for an elegant black-tie wedding or an anniversary at a fancy restaurant as you would for an outdoor barbecue or an engagement party at a friend's home. Just as your fashion is an outward expression of you, so too is your paper—from stationery to cards and, of course, gift wrap.

## Materials You Will Need

With such an amazing selection of papers, ribbons, trims, and other embellishments to choose from in the marketplace, how does one narrow the choices down? And what are the best tools to use to achieve a perfect, professional-looking package every time?

Although commercial gift wrap can be used to stunning effect, and is certainly appropriate for all the techniques in this book, my preference is to seek out unusual papers found in art stores, small stationery stores, and paper boutiques. It is in these places that one is bound to find interesting materials to wrap with, many of which are handmade, such as Nepalese lokta, Thai unryu, Indian wax banana, Japanese yuzen, Egyptian papyrus, and Mexican bark papers. (See the following pages for more information on these handmade papers.) I also like to shop at larger mass-market stores to find basic utilitarian elements such as brown kraft paper, rolls of solid-colored papers, and cotton string. One last place I love to source wrapping ingredients, and probably the most important, is my own home—wax paper, brown paper bags, newspapers, and magazines can all have a second life when transformed into a gift wrap.

Of course, no package is complete without an embellishment. Ribbons, ties, and gift toppers combine unexpected colors and textures together and give you an opportunity to accent the chosen gift wrap. From the simplest twines and ribbons to decadent jeweled beads and voluptuous florals to the quiet, honest beauty of nature, adding ribbons and embellishments to a gift is akin to putting the icing on a cake. I keep a drawer full of ribbons and trims, as well as a drawer full of stones, seed pods, leaves, and other findings from nature walks and everyday life. It is a treat for me to open these drawers and be greeted with myriad objects, colors, and textures. I wholeheartedly suggest finding a space where you can keep your own collection of ribbons, trims, and embellishments. It can look like many different things—a special box or series of boxes, a drawer, even an entire closet (if you have the space!). You will soon discover that it is like having your own treasure chest.

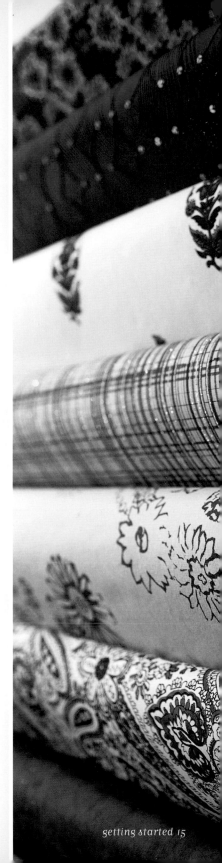

**Choosing Paper**

When choosing a paper for wrapping, look for one that is sturdy but not too thick; it should easily form clean, crisp edges and neat corners. The weight of a paper can help you determine whether it will be well suited for wrapping. Because most decorative papers are produced internationally, their paper weights are given using the metric system convention of grams per square meter (gsm). Lightweight or medium-weight papers, 18–80gsm, are ideal for gift wrapping. Papers greater than 80gsm tend to be thick, stiff, and bulky, making them more likely to crack as you make folds and creases; furthermore, thick paper can add unattractive bulk when numerous folds are required. Coated papers often behave similarly, and it is difficult to conceal their undersurface, typically a plain white color. Still, some thick papers, such as tree-free cotton rag, will wrap beautifully despite their high gsm (80–100). As you become more familiar with noncommercial wrapping papers, let your hands be your guide.

At the other end of the spectrum are ultralightweight papers, such as tissue, lightweight Nepalese lokta, and Thai unryu. When wrapping a ball or an odd-shaped gift, consider using one of these soft, thin, and pliable papers. These papers are more forgiving and are thus ideal papers to "shape" around an object.

The projects in this book focus on the wonders that can be achieved with whatever types of papers appeal to you. There are examples of how to wrap with everything from exquisite lace paper to ubiquitous brown kraft paper. Make substitutions as you like, to incorporate the techniques to suit your own sense of style. To get you started, here are some of the many papers I use in this book:

- - - - - - - - - - - - - - - - - - - - - - - - - - - - - - - - - - - - - - - - - - - - - - - - - - - -

**handmade papers**  Any paper made by hand will bear the mark of the artists and craftspersons who created it; truly, each sheet is one-of-a-kind. The papers listed here are typically found in art and craft shops, and are used for myriad projects—bookbinding, lampshade making, collage, card making, home decor, scrapbooking, and, of course, for gift wrapping.

- **katazome-shi** (35gsm) These decorative papers originate from Japan and are based on traditional kimono-printing techniques. The word *katazome-shi* literally means "stencil-dyed papers." Also referred to as *wazome*.

- **mexican amate bark** (150gsm) This sturdy handmade paper from Mexico is made from several different trees to achieve different colors. The bark of the jonote tree produces a coffee color, the bark of the mulberry tree produces a silvery-beige color, and the zalama limón tree produces a pure white color. Though it can be a little thick to wrap with, this gorgeous paper is a nature-lover's dream. Its texture and mottled color can sometimes be equated with leather.

- **nepalese lokta** (20–30gsm and 40–60gsm) This handmade paper is made from the bark of the lokta, or *Daphne papyracea*, a shrub that grows in the forest areas of the foothills of the Himalayas. The pulp yields a strong finished paper with long fibers and an attractive "crisp" quality due to its burnished, smooth surface. It is available in vivid earth tones, solids, and spectacularly blended colors.

- **thai unryu** (25gsm) This intrinsically beautiful paper from Thailand is made from kozo, or mulberry, fibers. Its translucency allows light to filter through the paper, making the long, swirling fibers embedded in the handmade paper easily visible. Widely used in the art world for collage, printmaking, and books, this lightweight paper is a delight to wrap with and is available in a range of vibrant and earth-toned hues.

- **tree-free or cotton rag** (80–100gsm) This is a paper made of cotton rag remnants resourced from garment industries. In some instances it may include agricultural residues and other recycled materials. Typically made in India, these papers are available in a wide range of silk-screened patterns from beautiful florals to ethnic designs to colorful graphics. These papers tend to be quite durable because of their cotton rag content.

- **washi lace paper** (*wa* meaning "Japanese," and *shi* meaning "paper") (18gsm) Washi lace paper is made of kozo fiber using the time-honored Japanese papermaking techniques developed by Buddhist monks in the year 610 CE, and is readily available in paper and art stores. Sheer and attractively patterned, this paper is commonly used as an overlay for invitations, wrapping, and home decor. Though delicate in appearance, washi lace paper is deceptively strong and resistant to tears, creases, and folds because of the long length of the kozo fibers.

- **yuzen** (35gsm) A handmade paper made of kozo bark. The word *yuzen* refers to a dyeing technique used in the kimono industry, and the paper's gorgeous, intricate patterns originate from exquisite textile designs, with intense saturated colors. Of the handmade papers, yuzen lends the most formal feel to a package and easily maintains crisp folds. This paper is generally found in specialty paper shops or art stores.

**decorative and specialty** From time to time, there are paper artists who come up with very unique new papers not seen before in the marketplace. This is always exiting! Papers such as gauze paper, paper-backed fabric, glitter paper, and fused metal papers are some specialty papers that I use for projects in this book. These papers can be more difficult to track down and are most likely found in small paper boutiques. Online paper stores are also good sources for unusual specialty papers.

**everyday papers** You don't have to wrap every package in a handmade paper to achieve beautiful wraps, and the papers in this category prove it. Often the best places to find these papers are office-supply and hardware stores, grocery stores, and newsstands—and maybe even your very own kitchen and recycling stacks! Even when you reach for commercial gift wrap and tissue paper; butcher, parchment, and wax paper; kraft paper and paper bags; or newspapers and magazines, by approaching your wrap with some of the creative ideas in this book, your packages will stand out from the crowd with wit and originality.

## THE RISE OF WRAPPING

*Paper as we know it today has its roots in Chinese culture. Its invention has been attributed to a Chinese courtier named Ts'ai-Lun, circa 105 CE, who created paper out of textile waste. The earliest form of paper, however, has its origins in ancient Egypt, circa 3000 CE. Made from the flower stem of the reedlike papyrus plant that grew abundantly along the banks of the Nile, papyrus became immensely important to Egyptian civilization, and it is from the name papyrus that we derived our modern-day word paper.*

*The original purpose of paper was communication, and paper was instrumental in the development of public and intellectual life. But paper was also used to package gifts, and wrapping gifts was considered a sacred art in both ancient Egypt and China. Later, this practice spread to Europe, where the first paper mill began production in 1085.*

*The Europeans created the precursor to modern gift wrap in 1509—wallpaper, although it was used as gift wrap only briefly because it tended to crack and tear easily. It wasn't*

*until the Victorian period of the mid- to late 1800s that the exchange of gifts between the wealthier classes brought about the use of elaborate and expensive materials to wrap with, including papers, fabrics, ribbons, and laces. Commoners used plain brown paper or tissue to wrap their packages, finishing them with string.*

*Today, beautiful handmade papers are available to people from all walks of life, though sometimes the simplest, plainest paper can make the most striking gift wrap.*

## Choosing Ribbons and Trims

Ribbons, perhaps the earliest adornment of clothing, became the province of only the wealthiest nobles in the sixteenth and seventeenth centuries, bedecking accessories, frocks, and even housewares. Today, ribbons are used frequently throughout our everyday lives, quietly nurturing our aesthetic sense of beauty and elegance. Associated with life's special moments, ribbons themselves have become representative of pride, promise, and celebration. Because of the many colors, patterns, textures, and sizes available to us, ribbons are a source of great decorative possibilities, embellishing our homes, clothing, crafts and hobbies, and, of course, gifts.

For some, walking into a fabric store or, better yet, a ribbonerie, is like walking into a candy store. Imagine spool after spool of luscious velvets, romantic sheer organdies, whimsical trims, metallic twines twisted in all kinds of patterns, regal satins, and hand-dyed silks all under one roof! A dream come true for many who believe that beauty can be found in the details.

Of course, ribbons aren't the only materials you can use to embellish a package. You may also want to deck out a present with trims like twine, string, fabrics, and bows, or even create a gift topper from objects and items you find and fall in love with in your daily life—perhaps a holiday ornament, a seashell, or even a spray of flowers. The options for embellishment are as limitless as your imagination.

---

**ribbon**  There are two major classifications of ribbon: 1) woven edge and 2) cut edge. As their names imply, woven-edge ribbons are woven on a loom and have finished edges, or *self edges*. Cut-edge ribbon is made from fabric that is cut into ribbon widths and then treated with a stiffening agent for body. Woven-edge ribbon can also be found wire-edged, or having a thin copper wire woven into the edges, giving the ribbon the ability to be shaped and to hold its body

• **grosgrain** A classic ribbon made of silk or nylon with a tight weave and narrow ribbing, grosgrain has a ridged surface. Because of its tight weave, grosgrain ribbon is very sturdy; however, its stiffness can be a drawback when manipulating the ribbon around the package, so grosgrain is my least-favorite ribbon for gift wrapping.

• **hanah hand-dyed silk** Made of 100 percent silk, this ribbon is characterized by a slightly tie-dyed effect achieved through its hand-dying process. This is my favorite ribbon to wrap with because of its gradations of color found within one spool, and is a source of inspiration in and of itself. It comes in widths that range from 7/16" (1cm) to 4" (10cm) widths, and in colors that range from intense, bright jewel tones to luscious, deep earthy colors.

• **organdy** Also referred to as organza, this ribbon is woven of fine synthetic fiber, usually nylon, and is beautifully sheer in its aesthetic. Generally available in widths that range from ½"-(13mm) wide to 4"-(10cm) wide, the color choices run the gamut. Because of its translucency, this is an ideal ribbon to pair with other solid ribbons, as the organdy then becomes a whisper of a color. Organdy can often be found with or without wire edges.

• **satin** Characterized by a lustered sheen, satin ribbon comes single- or double-faced, meaning the sheen appears either on one side or on both sides. For gift wrapping, I prefer the double-faced satin because it is easier to work with, since you don't have to worry about whether the ribbon is right side up. Satin can often be found with or without wire edges.

• **velvet** Made of either 100 percent rayon or 100 percent silk, velvet ribbons are sensuous to the touch and, because of the nature of velvet's soft pile, its colors are rich and intense. One of the most luxurious of ribbons, both in sight and touch, velvet ribbons are typically available with the soft pile on one face only, and can be found printed, flocked, or backed with satin.

## STAYING ORGANIZED

*One of the things that inspires me most and encourages creativity is an organized wrap station where I have the ability to see all that I have. Think of it as if you had your own paper store. It would include a collection of interesting papers perhaps draped over wooden dowels attached to a wall, with separate boxes for tools, ribbons, and findings. You may decide to hang your ribbons in a visually pleasing order of color, draped over a piece of string tacked at both ends against a wall. Another ribbon storing option if you have spools of ribbon is to create a wooden holder out of a dowel attached to a base, which could then be attached to a wall, preferably at a slight upward angle, or made for a tabletop. Should you have limited space, earmark a drawer in which to store all your wrapping materials and tools, or dedicate a large, flat box as a wrap station that can be stored underneath your bed. Whatever you decide to do, treat your wrap station like a creative playground and have fun with it!*

**other trim** Ribbon, a type of trim, is certainly not the only material to use when embellishing a package. There are numerous other options, many of which are ubiquitous, everyday items.

• **embroidery thread** Available in a wide range of colors, embroidery thread may be a humble tying material, but it can accentuate a package with its quiet grace. I love using embroidery thread with smaller gifts that call for intimate detail.

• **metal twine** This decorative trim is available in thread-thin widths as well as multiply twists. I always have a stash of gold and silver twine lying around, as I find so many creative uses for this material—from tying on gift tags to decorating a package, perhaps by securing a photo underneath (page 108). You will find that I refer to it repeatedly throughout my upcoming projects.

• **raffia** Raffia is made of paper or rayon. Though both raffias exude a rustic look, appearing sometimes like long pieces of straw, paper raffia has a more natural aesthetic and comes in nature-inspired colors, whereas rayon raffias usually come in brighter colors.

• **utility twine** Cotton string, thin rope, and utility cords are all tying materials that fall under this category. If you keep your eyes open, you can find unique things to create with in places like hardware stores and mass market stores!

• **wax twine** This thin multiuse tying material is available in bright and neutral colors. Typically used by pastry and sweet shops to tie up packages, wax twine is ideal for gift wrapping and makes a great color accent. I do not recommend using wax twine with a glossy paper, however, as the wax coating will leave a residue.

• **yarn** Yarn is a wonderful trim option as it comes in an overwhelming array of colors, from pale pastels to intense velvety darks; weights from super fine to super bulky; and types, from organic wool to fuzzy mohair to neon acrylic. Not only is the selection superior, but yarns are a comparatively economical tying material.

**basic gift-wrap tools** As with any creative project, you will need basic tools to execute professional-looking gift wraps. In a pinch, we can all be creative and resourceful and hand-tear paper rather than cut it with a pair of scissors, or omit the use of tape and simply use ribbon or string to hold the package together. However, the following items are helpful tools within the art of gift wrapping and will make your wrapping projects easier, and therefore more fun. Most are common to the average household. Less common tools are available in art, craft, office supply, or sewing stores.

• **tape** Both clear cellophane and transparent tape are suitable for wrapping gifts, though I prefer clear cellophane, as it has stronger adhesion and is more effective with handmade papers. Cellophane comes in two forms, as double-side and single-side tape. I prefer double-side tape as it enables me to create a cleaner finished look than single-side tape, since double-side tape can be hidden between the layers of paper. It is applied to the undersides of created paper flaps, thus allowing for the flaps to adhere to the tape's adjoining surface. It is available in ½" (13mm) and ¾" (2cm) widths.

Single-side tape can be used for general gift wrapping, but try incorporating the tape as a design element (pages 42 and 66). If you are going to see the tape, let it become an integral part of the design. This tape is available in narrow ½" (13mm) or ¾" (2cm) widths, as well as wider widths like 3" (7.5cm) wide packing tape.

• **tape dispensers** Although household-use tape dispensers are readily available and already stocked with a roll of tape, I recommend investing in a heavy-duty single- or double-roll model. Because the dispenser's heavy base keeps it grounded on the work surface, cutting a piece of tape becomes a one-hand operation, thus increasing your effectiveness in wrapping. Also in the marketplace is a pop-up tape dispenser that fits around the wrist with an elastic band, allowing for one-hand tape dispensing. This is a terrific tool for those who prefer to use single-side tape.

• **glue** Although glue sticks can be used effectively for light adhesion, I suggest using liquid all-purpose white glue applied with a small paintbrush for the projects in this book. In some cases watered-down glue is preferred; this is created by mixing one part water with two parts glue. When heavy-duty adhesion is necessary, reach for a hot-glue gun. The hot glue dispensed from the gun creates a strong bond between a wide range of materials—from fabrics to paper to found objects. This type of glue is ideal when creating gift toppers and is available in most craft or sewing stores.

• **scissors and cutting knife** Regular household scissors are sufficient for cutting gift wrap and ribbons. The sharper the blades, the easier and cleaner the cut will be. When an exact measurement is called for, I recommend using a cutting knife paired with a cutting mat and a metal straight-edge ruler.

• **cutting mat** A cutting base made of pliable plastic that is able to withstand the point of a sharp blade ensures a clean, smooth cutting surface. Available in small- to table-sized formats, these cutting mats come with a helpful visual measuring grid that encourages precise measuring and cutting.

• **straight-edge ruler** Made of wood, plastic, or metal, straightedges are available in sizes ranging from 6" to 36" (15–91cm) in length. I recommend a metal 18" (45.5cm) straightedge because many papers, particularly handmade ones, come in a standard 18" (45.5cm) width. I prefer metal rulers because cutting blades will not penetrate the metal edges, whereas plastic and wood are easily deformed by a sharp cutting blade. You can find metal rulers at art stores.

• **bone folders** Often recommended in paper crafts, bone folders are used for many purposes, including folding creases, burnishing papers, and scoring paper stock. A bone folder's smooth surface imparts a glossiness when drawn across a paper fold or crease, creating a more professional and polished finish than can typically be achieved by simply pressing the fold with the fingers.

Classic bone folders are carved from real animal bones, but today many are crafted from other materials. The ends of a bone folder are rounded with a point at one end for working in corners, causing the folder to somewhat resemble a tongue depressor. The pointed end is ideal for scoring, or creasing, paper. When scoring, I recommend placing a cutting mat underneath the paper; its slightly soft surface gives just enough for the bone folder to create a deep crease or score line.

• **sewing machine** A wonderfully creative tool with an uncommon application in the world of paper, the sewing machine is ideal to create paper pouches, adhere photos or flat materials to paper, and combine two or more pieces of paper. Always use lightweight papers and materials for best results, and have fun playing with contrasting thread colors and the multitude of decorative stitches commonly found on sewing machines.

• **sewing needle** Used with thread to make creative garlands (page 126), sewing needles can be used to create embellishments for packages. Hand-sewing with needle and thread is also a fine substitute for projects that call for the use of a sewing machine.

# WRAPPING YOUR PACKAGE

NOW THAT WE HAVE GONE THROUGH THE BASIC ELEMENTS NEEDED FOR GIFT WRAPPING,
IT IS TIME TO WALK YOU THROUGH THE PROCESS OF WRAPPING A PACKAGE.

I like to approach each item that is to be wrapped with a few questions. How can I enhance the nature of this object that I am about to give and make it personal for the gift recipient? How can I put a polish to this gift to lift its stature? In the following section, I share with you fundamental prepping, wrapping, and embellishing techniques that will become the foundation for every package you wrap and the basis for every project in this book.

## Prepping Paper for the Perfect Wrap

To achieve perfect or near-perfect wraps, you'll need to measure the paper before you begin. Each package will have different dimensions, so I have provided measuring guidelines that will ensure you start each wrap with just enough paper to do the job. In addition, prepping the paper with careful measuring will prevent waste; this is especially important if you are using a favorite or expensive paper, as there is nothing more disheartening than to begin wrapping a package only to find that your paper was cut just a little too short to cover your item. Once you've mastered these basic techniques, measuring paper will become quick, easy, and an almost subconscious first step.

### Measuring for the Basic Box Wrap (page 26)
**Paper Length: (Width x 2) + (Depth x 2) + 2" (5cm)**
**Paper Width: Length + Depth + 2" (5cm)**

To measure length, place the box in the paper's center. If the paper is on a roll, estimate where you think the center should be, and do not trim until completing this measurement process.

Bring up both ends of the paper, loosely "wrapping" the length around the box, meeting the ends at the center, estimating an additional 2" (5cm). Cut here to get the length of the paper.

Now, to measure the width, begin by again placing the box in the center of the paper. Bring up one width edge of the paper, allowing it to extend approximately 2" (5cm) beyond the top edge of the box. Lightly crease the paper against the bottom edge opposite this 2" (5cm) overage. Cut the paper along this crease to make the perfect width paper to wrap the box.

## Measuring for the Diagonal Wrap (page 28)
**(Length of longest side x 1.5) + (Depth x 2)**

Since this wrap is often used for thin objects like books or CDs, increase the ideal paper size incrementally if the package is greater than 1" (2.5cm) thick.

## Measuring for the Cylinder Wrap (page 29)
**Paper Length: Circumference + 2" (5cm)**
**Paper Width (height of cylinder): Width + (diameter x 1.5)**

To measure length, place the cylinder on its side at one edge of the paper. Roll the cylinder and paper, measuring a paper length that covers the cylinder's circumference plus an additional 2" (5cm). Cut the length of the paper. The width of the paper should measure the width (or height) of the cylinder plus ½ the diameter measurement.

---

### TOP THREE GIFT WRAP TIPS

*We can all use expert tips, and in my years of wrapping packages at Soolip, I have picked up a few tricks that can help create the best-looking gift wrap possible. These are tips that professionals use, and I guarantee not only that your friends and family will be impressed but that you will be delighted with the outcome.*

*1. Use double-side tape. Nothing looks nicer and more finished than a clean package without the tape showing, unless of course the tape is being used as a decorative element. Double-side tape should be affixed to the inside of each flap that is to be taped down.*

*2. Banish air bubbles. As you wrap your packages, hug the paper close to the gift box itself, constantly caressing out any air pockets. The palms of your hands should always be engaged in creating weight on the paper as you wrap.*

*3. Create the sharpest folds possible. Use a bone folder to crease folded edges before you tape them down. Once you've wrapped your package, give it a final, finished touch by pinching your thumb and index finger together at the corners. Run this pinch along all edges of the box, creasing as you go.*

## BASIC BOX WRAP

Undoubtedly the most common of all wraps, the Basic Box Wrap, when mastered, will carry you through many of the projects in this book. This wrap acts as a good foundation for ribbons and other embellishments, and comes in handy for all those presents that come ready to wrap in boxes of their own. In addition, any odd-shaped object that has you stumped as to how it should be gift-wrapped can be put in a box and then wrapped.

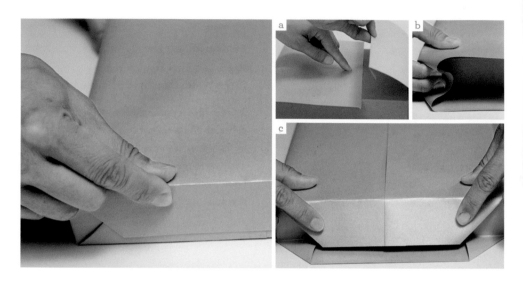

1. Place your box upside down in the middle of the paper. This will ensure that the final seam of the wrap will appear on the bottom of the wrapped package. If the box is a rectangle (and not a square), the length of the box should be perpendicular to the length of the paper.

2. Fold in one edge of the paper's length about ¾" (2cm) and crease. Using double-side tape, place a piece of tape as close to the folded inside edge as possible. (Single-side tape can be adhered to the folded outside edges, rather than inside edges.)

3. Place the opposite unfolded edge of the paper flat against the top of the box, using one hand to anchor it. Then bring up the folded edge against the top of the box and secure it by pressing down on the tape edge. As you do so, make certain that the paper is taut against all surfaces of the box. a

4. With the folded edge now secured on the top of the box, it is time to finish off the width of the paper, or the box ends. Begin by folding the sides inward toward the box. b

5. Crease folds close to the corners created by the box surface and paper.

6. Fold down and crease the top flap at both ends. (Since the box is upside down, this first fold creates the bottom flap of the final wrapped package.) c

7. Fold up and crease the final flaps that rest on your work surface. If you are wrapping a rectangular box, as shown, these flaps will have a flat edge. For each end, fold this flat edge in by ¼" (6mm) and crease. Then, apply double-side tape on the inside flap and adhere to the box's side, as you did in step 2. If you are wrapping a cube, the flaps should make perfect triangles with clean points. Simply affix a piece of double-side tape on each interior side of the triangle's points and adhere to the box's sides. Pinch the edges of the box on all sides.

## multi-sheet wrap

Whether your goal is to create one large sheet with which to wrap a particular gift or you simply want to combine colors or patterns of paper, glue or double-side tape can be used to adhere two or more sheets of paper together. This technique could be used to create a patchwork of paper, a wide stripe pattern, or any other combination you can design.

Apply the glue or double-side tape along the top of the entire length of one side of one piece of paper. a Then, layer the second piece of paper over the adhesive by approximately ½"–¾"(13mm–2cm) and press firmly. b Continue to add additional sheets as needed. You can wrap with this sheet as you would with any other paper; however, it's best not to place the seams joining multiple sheets along the package edges, because extra strain at these points may cause rips or tears.

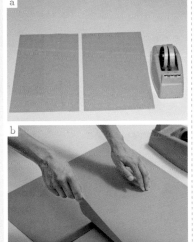

## DIAGONAL WRAP

The Diagonal Wrap is best suited for thin objects or flat shapes such as CDs, books, or shallow boxes, and is quite forgiving when it comes to the exact size of paper needed; many times you will be able to wrap an object with this method when your paper is too small for a Basic Box Wrap. For best results, cut a square-shaped piece of paper for the Diagonal Wrap.

*TIP: This method is ideal when you don't have quite enough paper for a full Basic Box Wrap. This wrap uses slightly less paper. I personally consider this wrap method to be one of my secret gift-wrapping tools because this method almost always bails me out when I am in a pinch for wrapping paper! You would be surprised how small the paper can be and still be able to complete the wrap! See page 25 for more tips on measuring the paper for this wrap.*

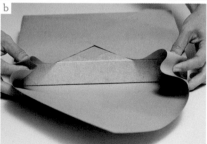

1. Place the box upside down in the middle of the paper at a diagonal. Orient the paper so that the bottom edge is parallel to your work surface.

2. Bring the top-left flap up and over the top of the box and crease the top of this flap edge against the side of the box.

3. Pinch in the corners you've created on this flap by creasing and bending the fold toward the side of the box, stopping midway. Do not fold the corners flat against the side of the box.

4. Lift the adjoining flap and fold it up and over the top of the box, taking care that the pinched folds made in step 3 stay tucked in place. a

5. Repeat steps 3 and 4 with the opposite adjoining flap.

6. Lift the final flap up and over the top of the box, pinching the corners inward as you fold. b

7. Affix one piece of double-side tape at the tip of this final flap and adhere it to the top of the box to secure the wrap.

**CYLINDER WRAP**  Mastering pleats and folds opens up a new world for wrap. Pleats are the perfect solution for wrapping cylindrically shaped objects like vases, bottles, and jars. When choosing the right paper for this technique, I recommend using soft, lightweight papers like yuzen, unryu, or lokta; the pleating folds will come out much cleaner. See page 25 for information on measuring the proper paper size.

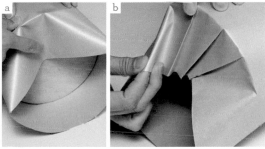

*TIP: The cylinder wrap is an ideal wrapping method for any odd-shaped, long, or narrow gift. If you are wrapping an odd-shaped object, consider creating a uniform cylinder around which to wrap. You can do this by rolling and taping a thin piece of cardboard around the circumference of the object, making the width of the cardboard 1–2" (2.5–5cm) wider than the width/(or height) of the object.*

1. To create a finished outer edge, fold in one edge of the paper's length ¾" (2cm) and crease. Using double-side tape, place a piece of tape as close to the folded edge as possible.

2. Bring up the opposite edge of the paper, rolling it around the cylinder, and secure the paper with the taped edge.

3. At one end of the cylinder, begin to pleat the paper ends in toward the center, by lightly folding down one side of the paper with your left pointer finger. Using your right pointer finger and thumb, crease where the paper naturally wants to fold. Continue to bring this fold down to the top of the cylinder, and at a slight angle to the left. Take care to keep the paper tight against the cylinder end, and remember to crease all folds. a

4. Repeat step 3 around the edge of the cylinder, overlapping each pleat as you go. b

5. The last pleat should appear as a triangle. Secure it by applying a piece of double-stick tape to the underside of the pleat and adhering it firmly to the cylinder end.

6. Repeat steps 3, 4, and 5 at the opposite end of the cylinder.

## Prepping Ribbon and Trim for the Perfect Package

To achieve the perfect length of ribbon or trim for any tie, I recommend approximating the amount needed. Of course, each package and each ribbon tie will require different dimensions. With practice, you'll be able to keep the ribbon on the spool and make a quick snip at the correct length—without wasting ribbon.

### Measuring for the Flat-Base Ribbon Tie (page 32)
(Length x 2) + (Width x 2) + (Depth x 4) + tail length

Loosely wrap the ribbon around both the width and the length of the box, allowing an additional 12"–24" (30.5cm–61cm) for a bow and tails. If a knot, not a bow, is desired, less ribbon is needed.

- - - - - - - - - - - - - - - - - - - - - - - - - - - - - - - - - - - - - - - - - - - - - - - - - - -

### Measuring for the Multi-Wrap Ribbon Tie (page 34)
[(Length x 2) + (Width x 2) + (Depth x 4) × number of wraps] + tail length

This ribbon tie is a variation of the Flat-Base Ribbon Tie, so estimate the length of ribbon needed in the same way; however, for this tie you'll need to do so multiple times, and then add the desired 12"–24" (30.5cm–61cm) overage.

- - - - - - - - - - - - - - - - - - - - - - - - - - - - - - - - - - - - - - - - - - - - - - - - - - -

### Measuring for the Del Rosario Tie (page 36)
[(Length x 2) + (Width x 4) + (Depth x 6)] + tail length

Loosely wrap the ribbon twice around the width of the box and once around the length, allowing an additional 12"–18" (30.5cm–45.5cm) for a small bow and handling.

- - - - - - - - - - - - - - - - - - - - - - - - - - - - - - - - - - - - - - - - - - - - - - - - - - -

### Measuring for the Ola-Hutchinson Suspended Object Tie (page 37)
2 pieces: (Width x 4) + (Depth x 4) + tail length

This tie requires two pieces of twine, each twice the width of the box, plus an additional 6"–8" (15cm–20.5cm) inches each for handling purposes.

## basic square knot

Various projects throughout this book call for a basic square knot, applicable for twines, ribbons, yarns, or just about any other kind of tying material.

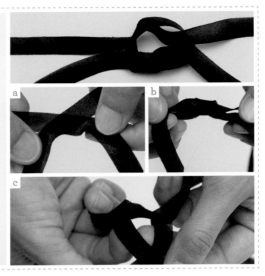

1. Holding one end of the ribbon in one hand and the other end of the ribbon in the other hand, cross the left end of the ribbon over the right, forming an X, and pull this end of the ribbon (now on the right side) underneath the cross of the X. a, b
2. Now, cross this right end of the ribbon over the left, forming another X, and pull it through the opening created by this second X. c
3. Pull taut.

## FLAT-BASE RIBBON TIE

This method of tying a ribbon around a box results in a clean, refined aesthetic. Since the cross of the ribbon on the box base lies flat against the box, the wrapped gift sits gracefully on any surface.

### wrap the ribbon

1. Hold one end of the ribbon at the center of the box with one hand, with about 6"–12" (15–30.5cm) (for the bow) extending beyond the center of the box.

2. With your other hand (referred to as the lasso hand) holding the long length of the ribbon, wrap the ribbon around the box. Be careful that the ribbon stays untwisted in this process.

3. Cross both ribbon ends at the center.

4. With the long end of the ribbon still in the lasso hand, wrap the ribbon around the box in the direction perpendicular to the first wrap, bringing the long end of the ribbon back around to the center of the box. a

5. Take the ribbon in the lasso hand and bring it to the right of the stationary hand. b

*The Soolip Fix*    *Adding ribbons to a gift is like adding frosting to a cake. It not only finishes off a wrapped box with an aesthetic beauty but also creates the intrigue that is intrinsic in the presentation of a gift.*

6. Thread the ribbon in the lasso hand under the intersection of the ribbon from the southwest corner up through the northeast corner of the box. c

### make the bow

7. Create a bow by making a loop out of each ribbon tail. d

8. Cross loops, left over right, and push the loop that you've crossed to the right side of the package over and back through the opening created by the loop crossing.

9. Pull both loops tight, adjusting the box if needed.

10. Either trim ends on the diagonal or create forked ends by folding about 2"–3" (5cm–7.5cm) of each ribbon end in half lengthwise and cutting diagonally from the bottom corners up to the ribbon folds.

## layered ribbon tie

I love layering skinny ribbons over thicker ones, as it gives me the ability to pull out multiple color accents from the gift-wrap paper, or to add another color to the look of the package. This tie is a variation of the Flat-Base Ribbon Tie. The only difference in this method is simply layering one ribbon on top of another and treating this duo-ribbon as if it were one. Have patience and take particular care to keep both ribbons untwisted and centered on each other as you wrap the box.

## multi-wrap ribbon tie

This variation on the simple Flat-Base Ribbon Tie was borne by last-minute necessity. Some years ago, I was on my way to a friend's house and picked up a gift at a nearby hardware store. But what would I use to wrap it? Combing through the aisles, I finally found some brown kraft paper and white cotton string. Unfortunately, a single wrap of the white cotton string in each direction looked a bit bare on the large box I had wrapped. So I wrapped the string a few more times in both directions, and suddenly the ribbon tie looked proportional to the box size. As a bonus, the triple strands of string running across the package both vertically and horizontally added an awesome graphic element to the package. Necessity truly can be the mother of invention.

This method is perfect when using a skinny twine or ribbon, particularly with a large box. By wrapping the ribbon multiple times, not only do you add a graphic element to the gift, you also create the illusion of an abundance of ribbon.

To create this variation, follow the steps for the Flat-Base Ribbon Tie (page 32). When wrapping the ribbon around the box, continue wrapping the ribbon two or more times around both the length and the width of the box. a, b Some adjustments may need to be made to the ribbon to space out the strands evenly. c, d As you tie the bow, keep in mind that when using a skinny ribbon it's best to keep the bow small and tight. Change up the look of the package by positioning the ribbon crossing at an off-center position on the top of the box.

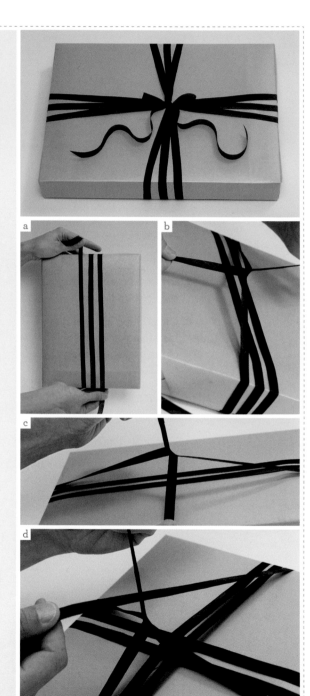

## ONE-SIDE MULTI-WRAP RIBBON TIE

We often think of ribbons and bows as big and exuberant, and they certainly can be. However, a ribbon tie doesn't have to overwhelm a package to dominate its look, and the One-Side Multi-Wrap Ribbon Tie proves this point with an aesthetic that is a step away from the norm. This tie uses multiple wraps of a skinny twine to create a somewhat ethereal and deconstructed look that is especially striking when fine metal twines are used.

*TIP: You can layer in photos, leaves, or a card underneath this twine "mesh." Look for more extensive projects utilizing this method later in the book (page 44).*

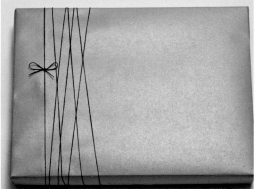 

1. Using a skinny twine, place one end at the top of the box, leaving a tail of about 6" (15cm) for handling. Hold secure.

2. Taking the other end of the twine, still attached to the ribbon spool (there is no need to cut the length at this point), wrap the twine around the box multiple times, crisscrossing the strands and allowing space between the strands to create a graphic element. a

3. Cut the twine and tie a knot or small bow.

## DEL ROSARIO TIE

This ribbon tying technique was created by and named after a talented paper artist and Soolip friend, Constantine del Rosario, whose clients clamored for a spectacular new look for their packages, one that would be simple, sophisticated, and anything but stuffy. Inspired by Japanese design, Constantine's creation reveals a particularly artful pattern that can be adapted to suit any occasion. Go graphic by combining a dark ribbon with a light wrap, or go smooth and suave by combining a narrow gold cord with a sophisticated yuzen pattern.

1. Fold the ribbon, leaving one side longer than the other by approximately 25 percent. Placing the fold at the center of the box, wrap the two ends around the box up to the top and thread them through the fold. a

2. Pull taut. Take each of the two ends, wrapping the longer end around the box, three-quarters of the way, to then "meet up" with the shorter end. b

3. Tie a small bow.

## OLA-HUTCHINSON SUSPENDED OBJECT TIE

Another particularly impressive tying technique developed for Soolip, this time by Soolip friend and talented calligrapher Billy Ola-Hutchinson, this ribbon tie doesn't just attach a gift topper, it becomes part of the design. You'll dazzle your friends with this unique tie, perfect for any gift topper, whether simple or elaborate. Twines and skinny ribbons are best for this tying technique.

1. Fold one piece of twine in half and, leading with the folded end, loop this folded end around your topper near its center, bringing the two open ends around the other end of the object and up through the loop. Pull tight. a

2. With the two open ends, wrap the twine around the box, bringing it up to the top of the box and under the topper at a point to the left of the first knotted loop, securing this with a knot, then trimming the excess twine. b

3. Repeat steps 1 and 2, wrapping the twine at opposite ends of the topper and tying it down to the box to create the tension needed for the topper to be secured.

## flat bands and pleated cummerbunds

If you are anything like me, you save all of your scraps of paper, as it is not only difficult but also wasteful to throw away any bits of beautifully colored, patterned, or textured papers. I have drawers full of paper scraps, rolled up and organized by color. Opening one of these drawers is like opening a box of new paints or colored pencils, and my creative juices just start flowing.

A marvelous way to showcase these decorative scraps is to make flat bands—perfect for showcasing ribbons or other gift embellishments—and their pleated cousin, the cummerbund, which is often decorative enough to stand on its own without ribbons. Bands and cummerbunds are also ideal for enhancing a handsome premade gift box.

For all bands, cut or choose a piece of paper long enough to wrap around either the length or the width of the package, depending on your preference, allowing a 1" (2.5cm) overage. The width of this piece of paper is versatile, depending on the size of the package and the desired look. In general I prefer the finished size of flat bands or cummerbunds to measure about one-third to just under one-half of the length of a package.

**To create a flat band**, create clean edges, if necessary, by folding them under ½" (13mm) along both of the long edges, creasing along the entire length. Use a bone folder to mark the crease; burnishing the folds is particularly recommended here. Then wrap the band around the box, affixing the ends to each other with double-side tape at the bottom of the box. Crease the band at the box corners for a crisp, tailored look.

**To create a pleated band**, create clean edges, if necessary, and then turn the paper wrong side up and fold up one lengthwise edge 1½" (3.8cm). Then unfold and turn the paper right side up. a To begin pleating, pinch this first fold with your thumb and pointer finger and press it down, allowing a ½" (13mm) margin underneath. b Continue to pinch each new fold and press down until you run out of paper to pleat. c For a piece of paper with a 6"–8" (15cm–20.5cm) width, you can expect to make about four or five pleats. As you pleat, take care that all folds remain aligned and parallel to one another. Attach the pleated cummerbund to your package as you would attach any flat band. d

*The Soolip Fix*    *Basic raw materials get my creative juices flowing. With everyday items in my hands, I think, "What can I do with this? How can I create something interesting, something beautiful?"*

## ribbon wrap over band

For me, part of being creative is being resourceful, and this method is ideal when only a limited amount of ribbon is available. It can also make use of scraps of decorative paper or ribbons and trims you may have saved from other projects. To prepare the package for the ribbon, simply wrap the box using one of the basic wraps, then add a flat band. Wrap the ribbon around the box and over the band one or multiple times, and tie either a knot or a small bow. If desired, add findings or beads to further embellish the gift.

# 02. ORGANIC & NATURAL

## A Touch of Mother Nature

*When I first began to pour my energy into wrapping gifts for others, I discovered that time and time again my presents seemed to draw on one theme—the outdoors. While not every gift I give literally interprets this theme, it is nonetheless my inspiration.*

Born and raised in Oregon, I grew up surrounded by nature—playing among the trees, floating down the Rogue River on my raft, and picking fresh blackberries in the summers along a nearby creek. As an adult, spending time outdoors has become a refuge for me. Long walks up in the quiet hills of Los Angeles let me unplug from my busy life for a few cherished moments. Free-climbing the smooth rocks of Joshua Tree National Park, ironically enough, has a grounding effect on me. Riding a gondola to the top of a snowy mountain keeps me humbled.

I am not surprised, then, to see this love for nature reflected in the wrapping I choose for my friends and family. Yet each time I decorate a package with a pressed flower or wrap a box in leaves that my children have collected from the yard, I am pleasantly surprised to discover that whatever element I've chosen becomes something new and different. The projects that follow all seek this transformation. You'll find ideas for wrapping with natural and biodegradable materials and adding natural embellishments that are really something special. Best of all, unique gift toppers such as these don't cost a thing. On your next walk around the block or through the backyard, look at your surroundings with "gift-wrap eyes." You may be surprised by what you find.

# PRESSED FLOWERS

Whenever I give a gift using this method of pressed flowers and herbs combined with regular packing tape, I always hear "Wow!" and "I never would've thought to use packing tape!" It's also a fun gift to give, as it always elicits smiles. Tape is such a versatile element, allowing you to incorporate and highlight delicate elements into a wrap.

## MATERIALS

solid-color paper

2" (5cm) wide cellophane packing tape

rounded, cleaned stones for handling tape

dried flowers and herbs

cotton string (optional)

tape

scissors

1. After wrapping your box in the solid-color paper (Basic Box Wrap, page 26), roll out enough tape to cover the area of the package you will be decorating with the pressed flowers and herbs. Lay the tape flat on your work surface, sticky side up.

   NOTE: I suggest weighing both ends of the tape down with slightly rounded stones so the tape stays put as you work with it. Using the stones as weights will prevent oily finger marks from appearing on the tape.

2. Carefully place the pressed flowers, or other elements, directly onto the tape, right side down and against the sticky part.

Take your time: Once you lay your elements down onto the tape, particularly delicate dried flowers, their placement becomes permanent. a

3. Once all the decorative elements have been placed on the tape, carefully lift the tape using the rocks at each end and place the custom-decorated tape on your package, pressing out any air bubbles. b

4. With the tape affixed to the package, remove the stones from each tape end and secure the tape firmly onto the package. If desired, adorn the gift further with string or ribbon, as shown. c

*wax banana paper*  These packages are wrapped in a wax banana paper. It is one of my favorite papers. I love the intense, delicious colors and the slight inclusions of the plant fiber scattered throughout the sheet. In addition, wax banana paper has a delicate crispness that reminds me of glassine, another favorite paper of mine. (I've been known to save the envelopes in which postal stamps are generally packaged to repurpose the glassine.) If you don't have access to wax banana paper, a good substitute is lokta, which is readily available in most paper and craft stores (Resource Guide, page 141).

# MICA GLISTEN

Mica flakes make an ideal embellishment to any project. In fact, the word *mica* is thought to have been derived from the Latin word *micare*, meaning "to glitter." Mica flakes were popular in the 1940s and 1950s in greeting-card manufacturing, but their popularity waned as more colorful man-made embellishments like glitter and sequins gained support on the craft scene.

Mica flakes originate from metamorphic rock called schist, and their slightly yellowed cellophane-like appearance retains a natural glistening quality, making them a perfect decorative ingredient with which to enhance holiday gifts. When applied using the technique described below, the effect often reminds people of snow and ice.

## MATERIALS

solid-color uncoated medium-weight paper

all-purpose glue mixture, three parts glue to one part water

paintbrush

shallow container to catch excess mica flakes during application (optional)

mica flakes (Resource Guide, page 141)

pressed foliage or a favorite photo

skinny gold twine

tape

scissors

1. After wrapping your box in the solid-color paper (Basic Box Wrap, page 26), apply the glue solution with your paintbrush where you want the mica flakes to stick. Apply the glue to the top of the box and allow it to drip down the sides to simulate dripping icicles. The more dripping, the better! a

2. Sprinkle mica flakes all around the package where glue was applied. If you missed a spot with the glue, or if you want more mica-flake coverage, simply reapply the glue solution as you work. b

   NOTE: I suggest placing the package either in a wide shallow container or on top of a large piece of paper in order to catch the excess mica flakes. This way, they will be easier to capture for reuse.

3. Allow the package to dry. Lightly press your finger on the package where the mica flakes have settled to test for dryness. Once the glue is dry, lay pressed foliage on top of the package.

4. Secure the foliage in place with the skinny gold twine, using the One-Side Multi-Wrap Ribbon Tie (page 35), wrapping the twine around the package multiple times. c

# A NEST OF TREASURES

It is so much fun to give this gift, a stack of beautifully covered boxes wrapped in three different, lively patterns and then topped off with an equally lively enchanting bird perched in her nest. It is almost as if the little bird is guarding not only the eggs in the nest (jelly beans) but also a treasure—the three stacked gifts. I love the anticipation that sets in immediately upon presenting this stack to a friend, and as each box is unwrapped, the excitement builds. This gift wrap is a perfect option for any spring event. As eggs represent birth, so too this could be an ideal embellishment for a baby gift.

1. To create the pouch of "eggs" lying inside the nest, trace the round shape of a bowl, approximately 5" (12.5cm) in diameter, onto the netting. Cut out the circle shape.

2. Place the candy in the center of this circle. Bring up all edges of the circle, holding the netting around the candy tightly with one hand. Tie the netting closed with a piece of seam binding and place this pouch in the nest, tied side down. If you feel a need to secure the pouch in the nest, use a longer piece of seam binding to tie the pouch and then weave the ends through the nest. a

3. Wrap your boxes (Basic Box Wrap, page 26) with your decorative paper and stack the set of three boxes (or more!), placing them one on top of another, with the largest box on the bottom. You may use a piece of tape between each box to hold them in place. Be creative with this project by choosing papers with different patterns, creating a more spirited presentation.

4. Measure out both colors of seam binding by loosely wrapping them twice around the height of all three boxes, allowing approximately 36" (91cm) additional excess for longer-than-normal ribbon tails. Wrap the seam bindings around the boxes using the Layered Ribbon Tie method (page 33), finishing with a knot rather than a bow. When complete, spread the two lengths of bindings apart. b

## MATERIALS

sheer netting

bowl (approximately 5" [12.5cm] in diameter)

scissors

jelly beans

seam binding, two colors

small nest

decorative paper, such as tree-free paper

tape

tweezers

bird topper

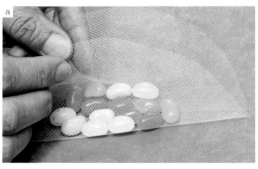

**5.** Secure the nest topper at the top of the boxes using a piece of seam binding, threading it through the bottom of the nest using tweezers and then around the ribbon intersection at the top of the stacked boxes. c

**6.** Finally, secure the bird just off-center in the nest. d

**NOTE:** Turn any object into a gift topper using thin wire and a little ingenuity. Depending on the shape and material, simply wrap the wire around a portion of the object or poke two small holes where necessary to thread the wire through.

My son Dag is a romantic when it comes to stones. He collects them all—large ones, small ones, perfectly round ones, unusually shaped ones, polished ones, rough ones. His obsession has not only opened my eyes to how beautiful and unique each stone can be but also inspired more gift toppers than I would have ever thought possible.

Use the instructions for the Basic Stone Wrap, below, as a springboard for your own Collection of Stones. More examples of stone wrapping techniques are provided on the following page. I often add multiple stone gift toppers to a package, as shown here.

### BASIC STONE WRAP

**MATERIALS**
(for all wrapped stone projects)

crimped wire

stones

wire cutter

narrow silk ribbon

scissors

moss

skinny gold twine

wax twine

wide silk ribbon, 2½" (6.5cm) width

hot-glue gun

1. Place crimped wire flat against the center part of a stone, allowing a 4" (10cm) tail to extend beyond the stone. a

2. Keeping the wire attached to the spool, wrap the wire around the stone, allowing the stone's unique shape to dictate which ribbon tie you use. (Here I've chosen the Multi-Wrap Ribbon Tie [page 34] with the wire crossing on the bottom of the gift topper.) b

3. Finish the wrapping with the wire meeting the 4" (10cm) tail. Trim the wire, leaving a 4" (10cm) excess, and twist both ends together to secure the wire.

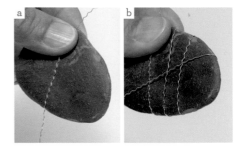

### COLLECTION OF STONES

1. Wrap the wide silk ribbon around a wrapped package or a gift box, as shown, in a uniform manner, beginning and ending the ribbon wrap on the bottom of the box.

2. Trim the tails of the Little Buddha, Stone & Silk, and The Gift wrapped stone toppers (page 51), or any wrapped stone designs.

3. Apply hot glue to the bottom of each topper and mount to the ribbon as desired. Let the glue dry.

**NOTE:** The basic stone wrap technique adapts to accommodate any size or shape stone. If I'm having a particularly creative, productive day, I'll often make up separate gift toppers like these so I'll have them on hand when I'm in a hurry and need a special wrap.

**Stone & Silk** Using a narrow silk ribbon, wrap this stone using the Multi-Wrap Ribbon Tie (page 34). Wrap the ribbon around the stone twice in each direction. Trim both ribbon ends close to the knot and thread a separate 8" (20.5cm) piece of ribbon around the ribbon intersection at the bottom side of this stone. These tails can be used to secure this gift topper to the ribbon of a wrapped gift.

**Wrapped Stone** A mottled gray stone shows off its unique personality with the Basic Stone Wrap technique.

**Moss Nest** For this variation, I've nestled a stone on top of a bed of moss before wrapping with the crimped wire. As with other wrapped-stone embellishments, secure the wire by twisting the wire ends together underneath the bed of moss.

**The Gift** This special stone embellishment secures one stone to another stone. Place a tiny pebble at the center of a concave stone. Then, using skinny gold twine, wrap the twine around the stones three times in one direction and three times in the opposite direction. Tie a square knot at the base of the stone.

**Little Buddha** To create this variation, wrap wax twine around the stone using the bundling technique from Bundle of Twigs (page 54). Once the stone is bundled to your satisfaction, wrap a separate 12" (30.5cm) piece of wax twine once around the middle of the stone and tie a square knot to the back, or bottom, of the stone. Leave 4" (10cm) tails to be used to secure the topper to a package.

*Once I've completed my Leaf Wrap, I like to use long, pliable grasses to create decorative ties around the package, thus keeping this gift wrap completely biodegradable. However, skinny twine or embroidery thread also creates beautiful finished looks with this wrap, as shown here.*

# LEAF WRAP

This is a creative way to wrap small items, such as a pair of earrings. There's no way this standout wrap will be lost amid the other packages. The key to wrapping with leaves is to choose those leaves that are supple and have a large, flat surface. Banana leaves, palm leaves, and canna leaves are ideal and can be found abundantly in warm places, such as my own sunny Southern California. However, these leaves can also be found readily in Latin American or Asian groceries, as both of these cultures use the leaves as wraps for food dishes. You can also source these leaves at your local florist. Alternatives to these warm-weather leaves would be large maple or oak leaves.

1. Place the leaf on your work surface and wipe down the front and back with a moist cloth, ridding the leaf of any dirt particles. This will also add a bit of moisture to the leaf, making it more pliable.

2. Position the earrings, or any other small item you may be wrapping, in the open area of the leaf and slightly more toward the base of the leaf. Using a toothpick or the earring posts themselves, poke two holes in the leaf at a comfortable but close distance. You will need the space around the object to complete the wrapping.

3. Thread the earrings through. If you are wrapping another type of object, there is no need to secure the item to the leaf. Allow it to simply float. a

4. Wrap the object by folding the bottom part of the leaf upward to cover the earrings, and then fold in both the left and the right sides of the leaf. b

5. Finally, fold the top side of the leaf down and around the back of the package, wrapping the excess leaf around the square shape as many times as necessary. c

6. Secure these folds by wrapping skinny twine around the package multiple times. If desired, add another leaf, flower, or other nature finding to accentuate your package.

## MATERIALS

large canna leaf or any leaf with a large, flat surface, such as a banana leaf

toothpick (optional)

skinny gold twine or long grass

scissors

# BUNDLE OF TWIGS

Like many people who balance work and family, I often find myself in a pinch for gift wrap. It's times like these that I take a deep breath, relax, and step out into my backyard, as I know that I will find something beautiful there, something that deserves to be the crown jewel of a gift, no matter how simple or common.

I've always loved the simplicity of a bundle of twigs. It resembles a stack of firewood ready for the fireplace or campsite. Thus, this gift topper is perfect for gift-giving in the fall and winter months.

**MATERIALS**

twigs

wax twine

balsa wood box

scissors

silk ribbon

1. Gather twigs. Break or cut them into similar lengths.

2. Group them in a bundle. Begin the process of wrapping the bundle with wax twine by laying one end of the twine along the length of the twigs, holding it firmly in place with your hand, leaving an excess tail of approximately 6" (15cm). With the other hand, begin wrapping the twine around the bundle at the opposite end. a

3. Continue wrapping the twine around the bundle and over the 6" (15cm) excess tail, taking care to keep the rounds of twine close and tight to one another. As you wrap the twine, the twine tail will become more secure underneath all the rounds. b

4. When you have bound the length of the bundle, trim the wax twine about 3" (7.5cm) from the bundle and tie a knot using the two twine tails. c

5. Wrap your gift box with paper, if desired, or use a wood box, as shown. Tie the ribbon around the box using the Flat-Base Ribbon Tie without the bow (page 32) and weave the two wax twine tails under the ribbon intersection, each weaving underneath from the opposite direction. Knot the twine using a square knot around the ribbon intersection to secure this gift topper.

a

b

c

*balsa wood*     The balsa wood tree is a relatively fast-growing plant native to Central and South America. Balsa wood is a sturdy yet lightweight wood, and is typically used in model making. You will find it readily in hobby and craft stores.

# LICHEN MOSS FILLING

The beauty of a distinctively wrapped package isn't just "paper-deep." You can really wow your friends and family with this idea for an all-natural packing filler, inspired by Soolip friend and gifted floral artist Sharon Lowe. Sharon always sees things in a unique way, and gift wrap is no exception. Tucking an element of nature (such as lichen moss, shown here) around a gift completely transforms the experience of opening the package from ho-hum to unforgettable. Experiment with other "filler" possibilities, such as green moss, pine or cedar boughs, dried flowers or seed pods, raw cotton, and bark.

1. Cut a length of wide silk ribbon that is long enough to line the bottom of the box, wrap around the gift, and finish with a bow. For my package, I cut approximately 36" (91cm).

2. Lay and straddle the ribbon across the width of the box center.

3. Line the inside box edges with lichen moss, leaving a space in which to nestle the gift. a

4. Place the gift inside the box, surrounding it with lichen moss.

5. Wrap the ribbon around the gift and tie a bow. Take care to not pull the ribbon too tight, as you want to refrain from pulling on the moss. b

6. Place a lid on the box and, if desired, add a single strand of narrow ribbon to the outside as a final touch. c

NOTE: If the gift you are placing inside is delicate or sensitive in any way, you may want to consider first wrapping it in protective tissue or cellophane

## MATERIALS
wide silk ribbon

scissors

balsa wood box

lichen moss

narrow ribbon (optional)

# 03. RESOURCEFUL & INVENTIVE

## Using What You Already Own

*I am so excited to present a chapter on resourceful gift-wrapping ideas. This is where a lot of my passion lies, as I feel that being resourceful with what we already have is fundamentally necessary to sustain our planet. Being resourceful is not only creatively challenging but also incredibly satisfying.*

Many of the ideas presented here came about because of my own last-minute gift-wrapping needs. At times, we all find ourselves at home without traditional, "proper" gift wrap at hand. The challenge is to think on our feet, grab what is available, see the materials in an inspired way, and of course give that package love!

In the pages that follow, I give you gift-wrapping ideas using common household materials—wax paper, kraft paper, magazine pages, copy paper. I'll even show you how to turn common kitchen plastic wrap into a fun, decorative ribbon! Economical and creative at the same time, I hope these ideas inspire you to use the everyday treasures that lie at your own fingertips!

# FROM THE GLOSSIES

Okay, I confess—I love flipping through fashion, style, and design magazines. I often marvel over the sensual brightly colored images, and I find myself yearning to use them in some way. In addition, it pains me to discard all that paper without at least repurposing some of it.

Due to the size of the average magazine, I use the Diagonal Wrap technique (page 28) when repurposing magazine pages. Keep in mind that this is an ideal wrap for smaller gifts, as well as for those that are fairly shallow. Of course, the bigger the magazine page, the larger the gift box it will wrap.

1. Tear out a page from a magazine. Trim the edges neatly.

2. Place the box at a diagonal on top of the paper, to the left of the center.

3. Bring the paper up and over the lower-left corner of the box and crease the corners inward. a

4. Repeat step 3, wrapping each flap over the box and creasing the corners in until the box is completely covered.

5. Secure the final flap with one piece of double-side tape. Finish off the gift with colorful embroidery-thread accents. b

## MATERIALS

magazine
(large-format
magazines are best)

scissors

tape

embroidery thread

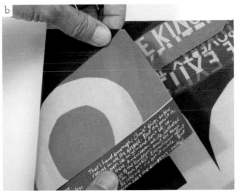

# WAX PAPER PLANT WRAP

Live potted plants can be a challenge to wrap, and one usually succumbs to using a simple ribbon and bow around the container. Nice and functional. However, when I give a plant as a gift, I feel the same way I do when giving a gift in a traditionally shaped box—adding a special gift-wrap touch is important. It creates the mystery and suspense that is part of the gift-giving experience.

## MATERIALS

live potted plant

wax paper

¼" (6mm) hole punch

two colors of silk ribbon

scissors

double-side tape

1. Place the potted plant in the middle of a piece of wax paper. The length of the wax paper should measure approximately 3 times the height of the plant.

2. Bring up 2 opposite sides of the wax paper to touch each other above the plant. a

3. Keeping these 2 ends together, fold the paper down 1" (2.5cm), crease, and continue folding and creasing at 1" (2.5cm) intervals until you reach the top of the plant.

4. Using the hole punch, make 2 holes in the center of the folded layers, each 1" (2.5 cm) apart. b

5. Cut an 18" (45.5cm) strand of each of the two colors of ribbon, and thread them both

through the holes. Start by threading the ribbons through one hole from the front of the package, through the back, and back to the front in the opposite hole. Tie a bow and trim the ribbon tails.

6. To finish off one side, lift up the bottom side of the wax paper that lies on your work surface.

7. Gently fold the back flap forward toward the middle. c

8. Fold the front flap back toward the middle and secure it with a piece of double-side tape to the back flap. d

9. Repeat steps 6–8 on the other side.

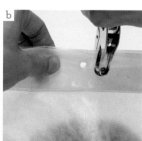
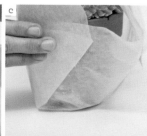

# DUO-COLOR SPHERE WRAP

Though most packages are easily wrapped in traditional boxes, others may be more of a challenge, and no shape frustrates would-be wrappers more than a sphere. Paper folding and round shapes just don't seem to go together! Indeed, children's toys often seem to be oddly shaped and can require, well, some thinking outside the box. To wrap round shapes, loosely imagine the sphere as a square.

**MATERIALS**

tissue paper, chocolate and green, or other colors of your choice

double-side tape

white shoestring

1. To create a duo-color wrap as shown, lay several sheets of the outer-color tissue on top of the inner-color tissue, with a 3" (7.5cm) border of the inner tissue exposed.

2. Place the round object on top, slightly below center.

3. Bring one side of the tissue up and over the sphere, wrapping it about halfway. a

4. Keeping the inner sheets together, fold their edges in about 1" (2.5cm). This will prevent any of the inner color from peeking out of this side seam.

5. Apply a piece of double-side tape between the inner sheets so they stay connected as you wrap.

6. Again, imagining the sphere as a square with four equal sides, fold down the top "side," and then fold the two perpendicular sides inward, creating a pointed bottom flap. b

7. Finish off the bottom of the gift wrap by applying double-side tape on this pointed flap and folding it up.

8. Setting this "box" on the bottom pointed flap, cinch the excess tissue at the top of the package and secure it by wrapping the white shoestring around the "neck" of the gift. c

*In this example my son Odin holds a basketball we wrapped in brightly colored green and brown tissue paper. I generally use tissue paper to wrap spheres because of its pliability. I used two colors in this example for aesthetic reasons and for strength.*

# COPY PAPER WRAP

Like many great ideas, this resourceful wrap was borne by necessity. About to head out to an after-work party with no gift wrap and little time, I used what was available—copy paper, packing tape, and the office houseplant. Fortunately, the wrap came together beautifully, and not only did my coworkers not mind the somewhat unusual use of office supplies, they were inspired to look around the office for other creative possibilities.

Though I have incorporated herb leaves as the decorative element of this project, any material that is relatively flat—sequins, bits of colored paper, flattened flowers, coins, buttons, stamps, pins, paper clips, and so much more—can be used.

## MATERIALS

clear packing tape

rounded stones or other weighted objects to handle the tape

about 16 sage leaves, or other decorative elements

four pieces 8½" x 11" (21.5cm x 28cm) copy paper (This creates a final piece of paper that measures 17" x 22" [43cm x 56cm]. If this is insufficient for the item you are wrapping, simply add more sheets.)

1. Roll out 28" (71cm) of packing tape and place it on a work surface, sticky side up. Weigh down each end using stones or other objects, such as staplers, paperweights, and water glasses, to ground the tape. If you are using more than 4 sheets, you will need to measure out a longer length of tape. Place sage leaves at 1" (2.5cm) intervals along the entire length of the packing tape. a

2. Roll out 23" (58.5cm) of packing tape, sticky side up, and place it on top of and perpendicular to the 28" (71cm) long piece to form a cross. Place sage leaves along the tape as in the previous step, orienting the leaves so they point in the same direction.

3. Carefully place the first piece of copy paper at the lower-left intersection of the tape, covering half the width of the tape at the top and right of the paper. Properly placing this first piece of paper is critical, because it will determine the placement of the remaining papers. Each sheet will share the width of the tape at this intersection. b

**NOTE:** Be careful with the placement of the paper, as you have only one shot!

4. Place the second sheet in the lower-right-hand quadrant.

5. Place the third sheet in the upper-left-hand quadrant.

6. Finally, place the fourth and final sheet in the upper right-hand quadrant. You now have a fabulous piece of paper with which to wrap your gift! c

## BEING ECO-CONSCIOUS

Of course, you can live "green" in more ways than one, and when wrapping presents inspired by nature or recycled materials, I often think quite literally—and draw on an earthy color palette. There are so many hues of brown, green, and gray to choose from! With variations of each from rich cacao to "barely there" shades of mushroom brown, from avocado green to powder-green cacti, from lush mosses to the soft shades of river rocks to the intense sharpness of charcoal gray, being resourceful and living "green" never has to be boring.

*An awareness and a respect for our Earth affects the decisions that we make every day, every moment. Most are small decisions, yet collectively our conscious efforts to not be wasteful, to reduce consumption in all areas of our lives, and to be grateful for what we have will be felt in the sustaining of our environment.*

*We can choose to repurpose brown grocery bags and turn them into gift wrap perfect for Kraft Paper Rubbings, shown on the following page. We can keep scraps of decorative papers, instead of throwing them away, and sew them together to make paper pouches like those shown on page 76. We can save gift wrap that we received from* *others, and reuse it for gifts of our own. And, of course, we can embellish packages with nature's treasures instead of purchasing premade gift toppers.*

*These, and so many more, are ways that we can act eco-consciously as we engage in the art of gift wrapping.*

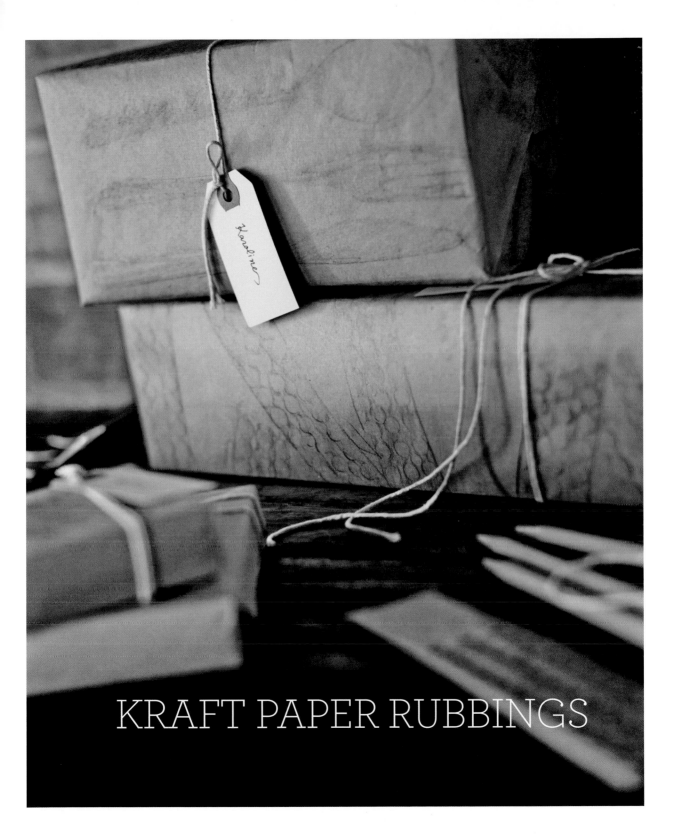

KRAFT PAPER RUBBINGS

The charm and peaceful nature of brown kraft paper and everyday cotton string could not be a more welcoming aesthetic, particularly in the busy world in which we all live. With that same spirit, I have used the ancient technique of rubbing to decorate the kraft paper, using graphite pencil and simple objects found around my home. This time-honored, rudimentary printing technique coupled with the pencil, paper, and string reminds me of my childhood days of simplicity and back-to-basics existence.

## MATERIALS

kraft paper

sharpened pencils

fork, spoon, and knife, or other objects

cotton string

manila tags

tape

scissors

1. Measure out the paper needed to cover your box. Loosely wrap the box with the paper, gently creasing the paper against all edges of the box. There is no need to use any tape at this point, nor is it necessary to do a full wrap or finish off the sides of the gift wrap. The creases are simply to give you markings for the placement of the rubbings.

2. Unwrap the box and place the paper onto your work surface, keeping track of which areas of the paper will cover which areas of the package.

3. Place the spoon underneath the kraft paper where you want to create the image. Using a sharpened pencil in one hand and holding the spoon in place with your other hand, lightly rub the pencil over the paper-covered spoon, taking care to create the definitive shape of the object. a

4. Remove the spoon from underneath the paper. Repeat step 3 using the fork and knife, creating the rubbings one at a time. Continue to add rubbings in this manner anyplace you wish the motif to appear.

5. When all the rubbings are complete, wrap the box with your paper.

6. Tie cotton string once around the box and complete the package by adding a manila gift tag. b

NOTE: When selecting items to rub and incorporate into this project, choose those with a lot of surface texture or an iconic shape, as they are ideal and well suited for rubbings.

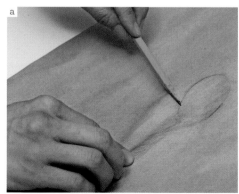

**Builder's Shim** This strange item is commonly found in any hardware store. The hardware store is full of unexpected treasures for this project and the result makes especially appropriate packaging for your favorite guy friend!

**Metal Florette** This project is the perfect way to incorporate any random findings that you may have in a stash of odd little things tucked in the junk drawer. The pattern on this metal florette lends itself easily to rubbing, evoking the blooms of a flower. I've reinforced the rubbing motif by mounting the metal florette onto a manila gift tag.

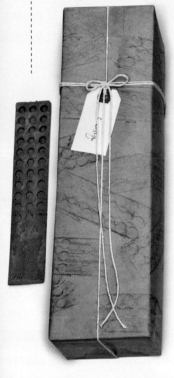

**Ginkgo Leaf** Again, leaves find their way into this rubbing. Leaves of all shapes and sizes, with their instantly recognizable shapes, are wonderful to use as rubbings. I love Ginkgo leaves and have used one here to create a rubbing on this square-shaped box.

**Botanic Garden** A pressed maidenhair fern frond sets the tone for this package. I have created four rubbings of this shape to simulate a fern garden. For added drama I used a carved stone butterfly, which I feel translates beautifully as a rubbing. Finally, the actual fern used for the rubbing is mounted on the gift tag, reinforcing the design.

# SHAVED CRAYON

Wax paper has such creative potential. Its milky, semi-sheer opacity heightens the sense of mystery and curiosity surrounding any gift it wraps. For this colorful wrap, I've sandwiched bits of shaved crayon between two pieces of wax paper, a particularly fun way to get the kids involved with creating custom-made wrapping paper. Over the years my children and I have created lots of different designs—some tailored, definitive shapes, and others wild and free-flowing creations. I so enjoy seeing the thrill on my children's faces when the towels are pulled back to reveal their newly designed wax wrapping paper. This is a perfect project to repurpose their old crayons in a delightful way!

1. Tear off two pieces of wax paper of the same length, large enough to wrap your present. Most wax-paper rolls are sold in 12"–13" (30.5cm–33cm) widths, so it is best to use this type of paper to wrap smaller gifts. However, you can always decorate the wax paper as follows and use it as a band (page 38).

2. Create colored wax shavings by sharpening the wax crayons, mixing wax colors as desired. Shave plenty of crayons so you have sufficient shavings to work with. a

3. Place one piece of wax paper on top of one of the towels. Wax paper generally has the same finish on both sides, so there is not a right or wrong side. Carefully place the wax shavings in the desired pattern on top of this piece of wax paper. b

   **NOTE:** Refer to Working with Wax Paper (page 75) for additional tips on creating wax-paper wrap.

4. Place the second piece of wax paper on top of the colored wax shavings. Take care in positioning this second sheet, as the colored shavings can move rather easily.

## MATERIALS

wax paper

colored wax crayons

crayon sharpener

two thin dish towels (Use old towels that you will not mind staining! The warmed colored wax can seep through the wax paper.)

iron

ribbon or other trim

tape

scissors

5. Place a second towel on top of all the wax paper layers. With an iron heated to a low temperature, apply heat on top of the towel at one- to two-second intervals, always picking up the iron from one spot to another, rather than using a continuous stroke. This technique will help keep the wax shavings from spreading out into an unrecognizable shape. c

6. Remove the top towel and allow the paper to cool. Now your gift wrap is ready to use!

7. Proceed with a box wrap and a ribbon tie of your choice.

### INSPIRATION

*WAXED STRING You can use the technique from Shaved Crayon to create wax-paper wrap with other materials. Here, I've used cotton string to create abstract art. In the past I have used a plethora of other elements—dried flowers and leaves, torn bits of decorative papers, sequins, photographs, and much more—to sandwich between wax paper. Colored wax twine or embroidery thread is also ideal. The only prerequisite is that the item(s) must be flat for the wax paper to seal properly. Once you've wrapped your gift with the wax paper, feel free to further embellish the package with crimped wire, ribbons, or twines.*

*working with wax paper*

Because wax paper tends to roll, use weights, such as small stones, to anchor the paper ends as you work on the design. Once the design is complete and you've covered it with the second sheet of wax paper and an old towel, place the iron directly on the towel for about 3–5 seconds (no longer!) and then pick it up. Continue this process, making sure to cover all areas of the paper with heat. Once you have done this and parts of the wax paper have melted onto one another, thus securing the design in its set place, you can feel comfortable making sweeping motions with the iron. (Never make sweeping motions when working with wax shavings.) This will ensure that your string, or other contents within the paper, does not displace as you are ironing.

# STITCHED POUCHES

My favorite design moments are when I come up with something that is not only visually appealing but also functional. These stitched pouches are just that—an innovative substitute for the box or gift bag and perfect for presents that must be sent through the mail. The post office can do its worst, as there is no bow or ribbon to squash. Instead, extra thread trails from these charming pouches for dramatic effect—and become the mechanism that allows you to tear open these gifts.

This wrap method is ideal for objects about 2" (5cm) deep or less. For ample room to accommodate your gift, measure the height and width separately, adding 3½"–4" (9cm–10cm) each, and trim the paper accordingly.

1. Using a straightedge and cutting blade, cut 2 pieces of paper each at 4" x 4" (10cm x 10cm), 5" x 5" (12.5cm x 12.5cm), 6" x 6" (15cm x 15cm), and 7" x 7" (18cm x 18cm).

   NOTE: The interior of the finished pouches will measure ¾" (2cm) less than these exterior measurements, so for larger gifts size the papers according to the dimensions of your gift.

2. Place 2 of the same sized pieces of paper together with the right, or patterned, sides facing out. Beginning at one corner, sew the papers together with metallic thread using a straight stitch, keeping a ⅜" (9mm) border. When you reach a corner, keep the needle in the down position (puncturing the papers), lift the sewing-machine foot, and pivot the papers so you can resume sewing the adjoining second side. a

3. Finish sewing the second and third sides.

4. Before stitching the fourth side, and while the papers are still on the sewing machine, place the gift in the pouch. b

5. Holding down the filled pouch firmly, stitch the fourth side, leaving 4" (10cm) thread tails. c

6. Repeat steps 2–5 with the remaining pieces of paper.

## MATERIALS

straightedge

cutting blade

cutting mat

assorted decorative paper

metallic thread

sewing machine

If you don't have the time to create Stitched Pouches (page 76), you can achieve a similar look by using premade paper lunch sacks. These charming pouches make ideal gift bags for party favors and small items. Consider doing this with a friend or with children, as you can easily create these bags in an assembly line.

*STITCHED BAGS Begin by cutting each paper bag in half. a One edge of the top half of the bag will need to be stitched closed before you place any treats inside. The other half, with the finished bottom, will need stitching only at the top of the bag. Before stitching, decorate the bags by gluing paper shapes and cutouts to the front of each. b, c If stitching both ends of the bag closed, as shown, stitch the bottom of the bag closed and then place the gift inside. d, e Fold the top edge of each bag down and then stitch it closed. f I use the zigzag stitch frequently, but feel free to try different decorative stitches to add varied looks to the pouches. You may also experiment with brown paper wine bags, especially if you have smaller gifts to enclose.*

a

b

c

d

e

f

# STITCHED PHOTOS

I am a nut for photographs and keeping archives of my family life. Back in the days of film photography I always requested the free double prints that film developers offered, both for crafting and for gift wrap. Now, I print my digital photographs at home, making this project more convenient. Because the photographs have so much life and color, I sew them onto a neutral background, such as kraft paper. For an even more economical wrap, you could also substitute a brown paper grocery bag for the kraft paper to achieve a similar look.

**MATERIALS**

scissors

photographs

brown kraft paper

glue stick or double-side tape

sewing machine

gold thread

1. Trim photographs as you like to creatively showcase your images.

2. Measure out kraft paper with which to wrap your box (page 24).

3. Create a canvas for yourself on the kraft paper by loosely wrapping the paper around the box and slightly pinching along the edges. a

4. Place the photographs on the kraft paper, using the creased lines of the kraft paper as a guide. When you are happy with the placement of your images, apply glue or a small piece of double-side tape to temporarily keep them in place. b

5. Using a zigzag pattern, stitch each photograph to the paper with the metallic thread, following the shapes of the photos. If you like, allow for long thread tails, as this adds to the overall novelty of the presentation. c

6. When all the photographs have been stitched, wrap the gift with your incredible wrapping paper.

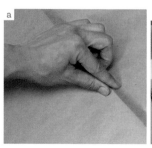

Creating a paper quilt out of small paper scraps is both resourceful and uniquely creative at the same time—an ideal way to incorporate favorite scraps of decorative papers in your gift giving and create an eclectic, curated look.

*nepalese lokta paper*

One of the most popular handmade papers, lokta paper is made from the lokta shrub, which grows quickly and bountifully in the foothills of the Himalayas. After harvesting the plant, papermakers boil, clean, and beat the plant with wooden mallets to produce a fibrous pulp. The pulp is then mixed with water and poured into paper molds made of bamboo poles and stretched canvas. The pulp dries in the sun, its long fibers tangling to form a strong paper with a crisp, attractive quality.

# SEWN PATCHWORK

A sewing machine allows for so many options in paper crafting. In many instances, paper can be used in ways in which fabric is normally used. Take care when using a sewing machine to use papers that are lightweight. This will prevent any possible damage to the sewing needles. Here I used two solid-color Nepalese lokta papers to make a duo-color patchwork sheet of paper against which the gift toppers could really pop.

1. To create an average-sized sheet of gift-wrap paper, measuring 20" x 24" (51cm x 61cm), cut thirty 4" (10cm) squares out of the lokta.

2. Visualize what you want the paper to look like by arranging the squares on a flat surface, 5 squares across in a row, alternating colors, and 6 rows down, also alternating colors.

3. With the sewing machine, use a zigzag stitch to connect 2 vertically adjoining squares, creating individual sections of two sewn squares. a

4. Connect all the individual sections together to create the patchwork paper "quilt." b

**NOTE:** You may find it easier to tackle one row at a time, stitching long rows and then connecting the rows together. c

5. Once all the stitching is complete, trim all excess threads. Use this paper to wrap the gift as you would any other paper, following the Basic Box Wrap technique (page 26) or another appropriate wrapping technique.

6. Using skinny silk ribbon, finish the gift off with the Multi-Wrap Ribbon Tie (page 34). Tie two bug gift toppers to each end of a piece of skinny silk ribbon and attach to the top of the gift.

## MATERIALS

lightweight paper, such as Nepalese lokta, in two or more coordinating colors

scissors

sewing machine

contrasting thread

skinny silk ribbon

two straw bugs, or other figurines to attach as gift toppers

tape

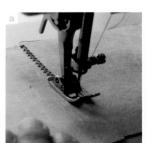

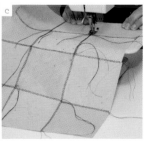

# CANDY RIBBON

When wrapping a gift for a sweet-toothed friend, use common kitchen plastic wrap to create edible wrap—candies become the decoration! Seasonal candies, such as conversation hearts and candy corn, top off a gift with wit and style. During the winter holidays, I gravitate toward the strong graphic aesthetic of red-and-white peppermints. At other times of the year I often reach for gummi bears, which are perfect for this project because their colors are clear, vibrant, and oh-so-charming! Using gummi bears, other types of candies, or even small objects will adapt this technique to gift-giving all year round.

## MATERIALS

kraft paper, or repurposed grocery bags

plastic wrap

peppermint candies, gummi bears, or other small candies

red skinny silk ribbon

red or white cotton twine

tape

scissors

1. Wrap your boxes in kraft paper using an appropriate box wrap.

2. To make the candy ribbon, tear off a piece of plastic long enough to wrap around both boxes, plus a 4" (10cm) excess. Lay the plastic wrap on your work surface.

3. Imagine the plastic wrap divided into thirds lengthwise. In the center third space, place candies in two rows along the length of the plastic wrap. a

   NOTE: Disperse the candies with ample space between each so the plastic wrap will adhere to itself, keeping the candies from moving around.

4. Fold the top and bottom thirds of the plastic wrap toward the center and press to seal. b

5. Wrap the candy band around the package. Because the plastic wrap sticks to itself, there is no need for tape. Embellish the gift further with red silk ribbon and red or white cotton twine. c

# LAYERED RIBBONS

Luxe and full of tactile interest, this resourceful gift wrap speaks to romantics. Surely, what is inside this amalgam of ribbons and trim is only enhanced by the thought that went into choosing the many materials of this gift wrap. This project is the perfect opportunity to use some of your favorite decorative trim remnants or ribbons that may have topped presents you have received in the past, as well as those you may have come across at a favorite trim shop or a flea market. A quick pass with a warm iron is all that is needed to refresh a previously used ribbon.

1. Wrap box, if needed.

2. Wrap the sequined trim around the box using the Flat-Base Ribbon Tie (page 32). Finish the tie with a half-knot instead of a bow. a

3. Wrap the crochet trim and the crushed velvet ribbon once around the width of the box, again finishing with a half-knot. b

4. Complete tying the sequined trim with one additional half-knot, securing it to the crochet trim and the crushed-velvet ribbon. c

5. In the same manner as in the previous steps, add the skinny velvet ribbon and the multi-twist platinum twine on top of the other ribbons.

6. Finally, affix the glass berry topper using a piece of skinny velvet. Wrap it once around the berry topper and once around the middle intersection of the ribbons. Trim the ribbon tails if needed.

## MATERIALS

dark wood box (or just wrap a box in a dark cocoa–colored paper)

sequined trim, 2" (5cm) wide

mauve crushed-velvet ribbon, 1" (2.5cm) wide

deep berry crochet trim, 1" (2.5cm) wide

dusty pink skinny velvet ribbon, ¼" (6mm) wide

multi-twist platinum twine

glass berry ornament

scissors

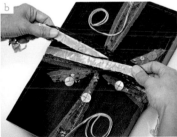

*The Soolip Fix*  *It is always a good idea to save remnants of items or materials, no matter how small or insignificant they seem. You never know when they will be the perfect accent to a gift or project.*

# 04. ECLECTIC & INTERNATIONAL

# Inspirations from Around the World

*At home and at Soolip, I am surrounded by unusual decorative papers imported from around the world, from the highly decorative patterns of Japanese yuzen and Indian silk-screens to the natural-fiber inclusions of Thai unryus and the crinkled surfaces of Parisian froissé and cloque. My introduction to many of these papers came when I was just out of college and toiling in the fashion industry. These years fed my appetite for and appreciation of color, texture, and shape, and also for travel.*

I have visited many places off the beaten path and, in the process, discovered new ways to enjoy and be inspired by the world—whether digging my toes in the clean sand in Baška on the beaches of Krk Island in Croatia; trekking through the Himalayas in Lhasa, Tibet; finding my way into underground music clubs in Havana, Cuba; working with craftspeople in Jaipur, India; or roaming through lavender fields in the south of France.

This chapter reflects these experiences—poetic, creatively inspiring, and aesthetically satisfying. You may have experiences of your own that influence your imagination, perhaps summers by the sea, a whirlwind tour of some European capital, or a visit to an exotic island heavy with mangoes. Perhaps you travel around the globe through novels and history books. So as you wander through the following pages, pay attention to the projects that call out to you. As you set out to create packages uniquely your own, reach for unexpected, eclectic, and maybe even international materials.

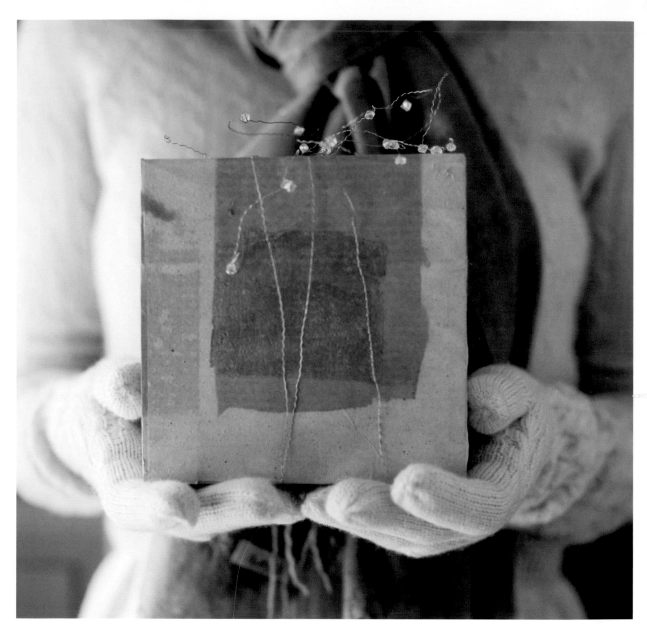

*joss paper*   To decorate this box, I used joss, a paper that has been a part of the fabric of my life since childhood. Generally found in Chinese stationery stores and Asian supermarkets, joss paper is customarily used for passing-of-life ceremonies. It represents money and wealth and is burned to signify the passing of wealth to the deceased person's spirit. Though my family never used joss paper in this way, I have used it to enrich my craft and art projects through the years. It was, and continues to be, another element found in my drawers of paper. Its rich orange and gold accents make it a particularly unique decorative component.

# TAMAYO JOSS
# PAPER COLLAGE

The distinctive wrapping idea shown here was dreamed up by the ever-so-talented Vanessa Tamayo, my colleague at Soolip. She has created this special wrap for customers who want a gift wrap unlike any other. Here, she has incorporated the joss paper as a collage element applied directly to a balsa wood box. Of course, tearing into a wrapped present can be part of the fun, so Vanessa has cleverly hidden a wire under the joss. With a tug, your gift's recipient can tear into this box without compromising the collage work on this reusable decorative storage box.

1. Wrap the crimped gold wire around the circumference of the box, just where the top and bottom of the box meet, leaving 4" (10cm) excess tails. a

2. Twist the ends once around each other to secure. Do not knot the two ends. These pieces of wire will act as a handle for the gift's recipient to open the gift with.

3. Use the paintbrush to apply the glue mixture to the entire back of a piece of joss paper. b

4. Adhere the glued joss paper to the box just next to, but not covering, the wire twist.

5. Place another piece of glued joss paper on the nearest adjoining side with 1" (2.5cm) of excess wire protruding above the top surface and beyond the side surface. Fold the excess paper around the corners they extend from. The excess paper folding around the side will want to cover the wire twist.

## MATERIALS

crimped gold wire

balsa wood cube box, found in craft stores

all-purpose glue mixture, three parts glue to one part water and paintbrush

Chinese joss paper (available at Asian supermarkets and Asian stationery stores)

clear faceted beads

scissors, or wire cutter

Gently allow the paper to tear around the wire. The twist should be exposed and sit on top of the paper. c

6. Cover the remaining exposed surfaces with glued joss paper, treating the corners as you did in step 5 and positioning the joss paper as you like. It is not necessary to place the paper only at right angles with the box; rather, you can overlap the paper randomly, being sure to completely cover the box. Allow glue to dry thoroughly.

7. Wrap the crimped gold wire vertically around the box multiple times, leaving 6" (15cm) at each end. Secure the wire to itself rather than into a bow. Thread clear faceted beads on the wire tails. To secure the beads onto the wire, hold the wire taut and simply twist the bead so the wire is secure.

8. Add 2 or more separate 12" (30cm) strands of wire and secure them to the wire intersection at the top of the box. Position a bead at the middle of this intersection and twist to secure. d

9. Add the finishing touch to this package by curling the ends of the 4" (10cm) tails on the side of the box as shown. e

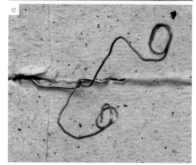

OBI-CLOTH BAND

I am a textile nut (in addition to being a paper nut!), and I love collecting patterned fabric, knowing that at some point the right occasion to use it will reveal itself. For this project I chose a traditional Japanese obi cloth, but I have used other highly decorative fabrics in the past, such as jewel-colored plaids or even those used for Indian saris. The louder the color and design of the pattern, the better. Remember, you are using only a narrow strip of this fabric, so a pattern that may seem too bold or over the top will likely translate into a playful, vibrant band.

**MATERIALS**

white glitter paper, or other decorative paper

decorative fabric

straightedge, cutting blade and mat, or tailor's chalk and scissors

hot-glue gun

contrasting piece of ribbon

tape

1. Wrap a box using the Basic Box Wrap method (page 26).

2. To create the band, place the fabric flat on a cutting surface. Position the straight-edge 1½" (3.8cm) along the edge of the fabric and trim with the cutting blade. (If you are looking for a little bit of stretch in your ribbon band, cut it along the bias of the fabric.) The ideal length of the band should equal the total circumference of the box, plus 12"–16" (30.5cm–40.5cm). If you do not have a straight edge or cutting blade, make trim markings at 1½" (3.8cm) wide with tailor's chalk and trim along the line with scissors.

3. Wrap the fabric-ribbon band around the box, positioning one end of the band at the top of the box. Apply hot glue to this end. The glue should be positioned at the center of the gift box. a

4. Bring the other end of the ribbon up and around to the top of the box 2" (5cm) beyond the center, allowing it to settle in the puddle of hot glue. b

   **NOTE:** If you want to make a bigger bow, simply extend this ribbon end farther away from the center.

**WRAPPING WITH FABRIC**

*The high number of available choices makes fabric a wonderful material with which to wrap gifts. Whether fabric is used to decorate a gift, as in the Obi-Cloth Band, or to create the complete wrap, as in the Japanese Four-Leaf Wrap (page 96), fabric lends itself well to creativity.*

*You may also take most of my basic wrap techniques demonstrated for paper and simply apply the principles to fabric. Hot glue will give you better adhesion than tape, but you can also rely on your own dexterity at folding and simply secure a given fabric with ribbons or twines alone.*

5. Fold the longer end of the band back over itself and apply a dot of hot glue to secure it to the ribbon already against the box. c

6. Continue this process, folding the long end back and forth, applying hot glue in the center of each layer to secure the folds and allowing the band to fold closer to the center by ½" (13mm) each time, thus creating a stepladder effect.

7. Finish the bow with the ribbon end at the center. Trim if necessary and secure with hot glue. d

8. Wrap a contrasting ribbon around the bow's center, securing it with hot glue. This will complete the bow. e

**NOTE:** The ribbon band is an ideal use for remnants of favorite pieces of cloth, perhaps from unfinished sewing projects, or worn, out-of-style clothing. Cut out as many ribbon strips as possible from the scrap fabric so the additional pieces can be stored and used at a later date.

# JAPANESE FOUR-PETAL WRAP

Inspired by traditional Japanese wrapping with the furoshiki cloth, this technique can make use of the multitude of decorative textiles available, from sensual materials, such as silks, velvets, rayons, and chiffons, to more everyday materials such as cottons and linens. Your choice of material, of course, will depend on the occasion and the character of the person for whom the gift is intended.

I find that the typical cloth dinner napkin, as shown here, is just the right size for many of the gifts I give. The bonus is that the napkin is finished on all sides, and is a piece that the gift recipient would use again.

**MATERIALS**

solid or decorative
piece of cloth

1. Prepare the cloth to an appropriate size. The cloth needs to be square, and the diagonal measurement should be three times the box's length. If the cloth is too small, the wrapped object may protrude out of the wrapping. If the cloth is too big, the end result will look sloppy.

2. Place the box at a diagonal in the middle of the square cloth. a

3. Take opposite corners in hand and tie them in the first half of a square knot at the top of the package. b

4. Lead the two remaining ends underneath the half-tied square knot and through to the opposite corner. Tie these ends into a square knot over the existing knot. c

a

b

c

*furoshiki*    Dating back to the Edo period, furoshiki, traditional Japanese wrapping cloths, were used to bundle clothes
while visiting the *sento,* or Japanese public baths. Eventually, this wrapping cloth served as a means for
merchants to transport their goods, as well as to protect and adorn gifts. Although furoshiki are still being
used in Japan, their popularity declined in the post-WWII period because of the proliferation of the modern
shopping bag. However, due to the recent awareness of and concern for the environment, reusable furoshiki
have experienced renewed interest in Japan and around the world. Wrapping the furoshiki way will not only
set your gifts apart from the crowd but also cut down on waste.

# GAUZE DECONSTRUCTED

By design, wrapping a present cloaks it in mystery. But sometimes it can be fun to tease a little, showing off just enough of the gift to pique the recipient's interest but not give anything away. In this case, I've wrapped this tray in a square piece of cheesecloth, a material ethereal, artistic, and readily available at most large grocery stores. A quick tea bath lightly stains and antiques the finish, turning the cloth into a retro-looking relic with a modern sensibility—perfect for pairing with the furoshiki wrapping method (page 97).

## MATERIALS

brewed black tea

square piece of cheesecloth or gauze, measuring from corner to corner approximately three times the longest side of gift

cut-out paper flower, or other gift topper

1. Submerge the cheesecloth in tea and let it steep for 5 minutes. The longer the cloth sits in the tea, the darker the cloth becomes. Remove the tea-stained cheesecloth and hang to dry.

2. When the cloth is dry, lay it out and place the gift facedown at a diagonal in the middle of the cloth.

3. Bring the top and bottom ends up to a point above your gift. a

4. Sandwich the two ends together and roll them until the ends are taut against the back of the gift. b

5. Bring the ends still extending from the sides of the gift up and around to the top.

6. Tie the tails into a square knot and attach the gift topper. c

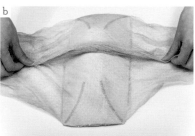

## INSPIRATION

There are many ways to achieve a worn look. Sometimes we make new wrap look old—like the cheesecloth we used in Gauze Deconstructed (page 98)—but sometimes we just use materials that have already had one or more purposes. This gift is wrapped in a piece of paper I stumbled upon in Paris, one that I have been holding on to for years, waiting for the perfect reason to use it. It is weathered, previously used, and (accidentally) water-damaged. I tend to think that these flaws actually make the paper more beautiful. Of course, crumpling a piece of kraft paper can approximate this effect.

*SERENDIPITOUS TEXTURE When using a distressed paper, it is a good idea to use more refined trimmings so the look doesn't stray into beat-up territory. This package is a good example of using design principle 01.—mixing high and low (page 9). Here I added a few remnants of decorative trim in a sangria-red and olive-green color palette to provide a resting place for this gift's crown jewels, the petite florette-shaped pods. Small dabs of glue at the center of each pod allow for a light powdering of gold dust to stick and sparkle. These pieces are then adhered to the decorative trim with hot glue.*

STARRY NIGHT BOX

The richness of gold leaf against the simplicity of balsa wood is a unique combination perfect for an extra-special birthday or for holiday gift-giving. For economical practicality I have used faux gold leaf, which may appear a bit brassier than real gold, but both kinds will remain shiny and lustrous. For this gift the gemstone topper links the precious metal to incredible jewels that occur in nature. This project will impress both at first glance and in years to come, as the gold-leaf box is itself a gift that can be adapted to many uses around the home.

## MATERIALS

all-purpose glue mixture, three parts glue to one part water and paintbrush

Japanese ribbon box or balsa wood box

faux gold leaf (real gold leaf can be used but is much more expensive)

soft, flat brush for burnishing

multi-twist platinum twine

narrow silk ribbon

gemstone, or other gift topper

scissors

1. Use the small paintbrush to apply a thin layer of glue to the box in the desired pattern, working with only a small area on one side of the box at a time. a

2. With one side of the gold leaf exposed by the interleaving tissue, carefully lay the gold-leaf sheet over the glued areas. Keep in mind that the glue must be moist for the gold leaf to properly adhere to the box's surface. Allow glue to dry. b

faux or real, with your bare fingers, as you will only create a mess!

3. Remove the interleaving tissue, then use the soft, flat brush and burnish down the gold leaf sheet with light pressure, making sweeping motions with the brush over the entire surface of the gold-leaf sheet. c

4. With the flat brush, lift one corner of the gold-leaf sheet and, with care, slowly peel it off the box surface. The gold leaf should stick to the areas where glue was applied. d

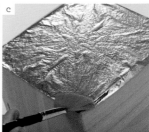

*The special* balsa wood box used in this project has slits cut out on all four sides of its base so ribbon can be threaded through the base of the box. The ribbon can thus remain a permanent addition to the box after opening, if desired.

5. Use the flat brush to brush away and remove any excess gold leaf. e

6. If there are areas where gold leaf failed to adhere, feel free to reapply glue and repeat the burnishing process in those specific areas.

7. Repeat steps 1–6, applying glue and gold leaf to each side of the box until the desired design is complete.

8. Tie the twine and ribbon around the box, using the Flat-Base Ribbon Tie technique (page 32). Knot the ribbon, but do not tie the bow.

9. Place the gemstone gift topper at the knot of the ribbon. Bring the twine and the ribbon ends up and cross them at the top of the gemstone. Bring the ends down and wrap them underneath the bottom. Tie a square knot to secure. f

10. Trim ribbon and twine.

# AROUND THE WORLD WRAP

When I travel, the typical tourist attractions are generally on my "to-see" list; however, the one special place that I make certain to visit is the local post office. I marvel at the amount of detail in both color and design contained in such small pieces of paper! Stamps can make great decorative elements for gift wrap, offering tiny lessons in history and geography, and sparking fun "remember when" conversations about special events and vacations. You can allow a single stamp to be the focus of a creative project, or combine several stamps by color or by idea to make a cohesive design.

1. Wrap the package with solid-color paper using the Basic Box Wrap (page 26)

2. Using the Multi-Wrap Ribbon Tie (page 34), wrap the string and twine around the boxes, finishing off with a half-knot or full square knot, instead of a bow. a

3. Secure the tails, if desired, by affixing the stamps to the top of the string and twine in a creative pattern. If the stamps' adhesive backing is no longer effective, use a glue stick to apply glue to the backs of the stamps to secure them to the wrap. b

## MATERIALS

lightweight or medium-weight solid-color paper

skinny cotton string

skinny gold twine

vintage, international, or other postage stamps

glue stick (optional)

tape

scissors

# SUSPENDED JADE

When it comes to evoking quiet opulence, nothing surpasses jade. Regal and compelling, this gem lends its noble heritage to any package it adorns. I've adopted an Asian-inspired style for the packages shown here because of jade's special place in Chinese culture. These gifts use handsome shades of green—kiwi, celadon, and deep moss—to show off the many shades found in the jade itself. From the mesmerizing jacquard-pattern paper to the intricate laser-cut red envelope to the detail in the carved jade object, the attention to detail apparent in each material makes this gift worthy of regard and respect.

## MATERIALS

decorative lokta paper

moss-green seam binding ribbon or raffia

carved jade piece, or other gift topper

gift card

tape

scissors

1. Wrap your box with the lokta paper, using an appropriate box wrap.

2. Cut one piece of seam binding long enough to go around the length of the box twice plus 8" (20.5cm).

3. Fold the seam binding in half and thread the folded end through the jade piece. a

4. Thread the opposite end through the loop created by the fold. Pull taut.

5. Bring the length of the seam binding around the base of the box and back up to the jade piece. Thread the end through the jade piece. b

6. Tie off the seam binding with a square knot and trim the tails.

7. Slide the gift card under the ribbon.

# ENCAPSULATED IMAGES

Gift-giving can be a way to speak from the heart to friends and family, and, as the saying goes, a picture is worth a thousand words. That's why it's easy to add an extra-special personal touch to a gift by wrapping it with favorite photographs. I often photocopy my photographs because their transformation from glossy color to grainy black-and-white can add an unexpected, abstract quality to gift wrap.

In this particular project I photocopied images of a wonderful day at the beach and attached them to the package using skinny silver twine. These randomly arranged strands of twine add to the abstract aesthetic of this package, which becomes a piece of art in and of itself.

1. Wrap your package in the decorative paper using an appropriate box wrap.

2. Hand-tear the photocopies around the desired images, knowing that imperfection here is welcome! a

3. Use glue and a brush to lightly affix the three images to your wrapped package. b

4. Using the skinny silver twine, wrap the package multiple times over the images so they are sufficiently enclosed by twine. With this particular box shape I wrapped the twine around the box from left to right, wrapped the twine back toward the left, and then tied the tails of the twine together toward the left side of the package.

**MATERIALS**

decorative paper

photocopies of three favorite photos

white all-purpose glue and paintbrush

skinny silver twine

tape

scissors

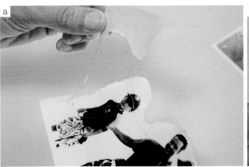

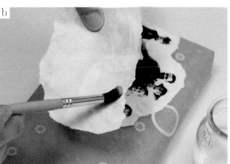

# 05. LUSH & ROMANTIC

## Sumptuous Couture Wraps

*To me, romance and luxury seem to go together, perhaps because both are qualities of life that are emotional, time-honored, and beautiful. For many of us there is no greater luxury than time, and channeling this precious resource into a gift wrap creates a wrapped present worthy of the most important events of our lives.*

From the paper pattern to the gift topper to the gift card, wrapping a package is akin to taking the time to get dressed up for a special occasion. Aesthetic consistency has a powerful effect. Fortunately, beautiful detailing need not demand hours of work, just appropriate design.

The projects I introduce in the following chapter all showcase looks appropriate to formal social settings. Yet these designs would also fit in at more casual settings, immediately uplifting any environment to which you bring them. These packages are delightful and inspiring whether you are off to a Sunday bridal shower in a fancy hotel or private garden, or attending a birthday party in a chic, modern restaurant or an intimate dinner for two at an upscale eatery. Join me in this chapter in celebrating the finer things in life.

# JAPANESE YUZEN PLEATED CUMMERBUND

This pleated cummerbund technique reflects the folding and tucking techniques often used by fashion designers to create rich texture and detail. For gift wrap it is the perfect way to use remnant pieces of decorative papers that are too small to wrap a gift but too beautiful to discard. Creating paper cummerbunds achieves a super-luxurious look, so when you want to splurge on an ultra-luxe paper, find comfort in knowing that you can spread the wealth to several gifts!

In many cases the pleated cummerbund is sufficient on its own as a gift accent, particularly when using patterned yuzen papers. However, go for extra drama with ribbons and other trims, as shown here.

## MATERIALS

solid-color lightweight paper

Japanese yuzen paper, or other lightweight paper

double-side tape

silk ribbon, 3" (7.5cm) width

scissors

1. Wrap your box in the solid-color paper using an appropriate box wrap.

2. Cut a piece of Japanese yuzen approximately 7"–8" (18cm–20.5cm) wide. The paper should be long enough to wrap around the width of your box with a 1" (2.5cm) overlap.

3. Fold in both long edges by ½" (13mm) to create finished edges, and execute the pleats as described in Flat Bands and Pleated Cummerbunds (page 38). a

4. Fold in one end of the cummerbund by ½" (13mm) and wrap it around the box, affixing a piece of double-side tape on the underside of the folded end to adhere to the other end and complete the band. b

5. Measure a piece of the silk ribbon long enough to wrap around the length of your box, adding 10"–12" (25.5cm–30.5cm). Wrap it around the box lengthwise and tie a square knot just over the pleated cummerbund. c

6. Trim the ribbon ends at an angle.

*japanese yuzen*     *Yuzen* is a term borrowed only several decades ago from the kimono-making industry in Japan. It refers to a type of dyeing technique used to decorate fabric for traditional Japanese silk garments, a technique invented by a man named Miyazaki Yuzen-sai. Yuzen paper is usually screen-printed by hand with patterns originating from exquisite textile designs. Like many handmade Japanese papers, yuzen is made from kozo, or mulberry, bark. Originally found in the mountainous regions of the Shikoku and Kyushu islands, kozo is now a cultivated plant and a major ingredient in paper- and clothmaking.

# MOTTLED METALLIC WOVEN BOX

If gold is, indeed, the metal of nobility, then chocolate must be the food most fit for kings and queens. It is no wonder that this gift exudes romance and decadence. A weave of mottled metallic gold paper covers wax banana paper in the deepest chocolate hue, making for a delicious presentation. Simple strands of skinny gold twine, almost invisible, focus attention on the glass berry gift topper and help create a color palette reminiscent of a box of dark chocolate–covered cherries.

## MATERIALS

chocolate wax banana paper

mottled metallic gold paper

straightedge, cutting blade, and mat

glue stick

berry gift topper

skinny gold metallic twine

tape

scissors

1. After you wrap your box with the banana paper, determine how many strips you will need to complete a weave. As a general rule, allow for a ¾" (2cm) space between each strip. Once you have the width and the length measurements, divide each measurement by 1.5. This will give you the number of strips you will need on each side. If you come up with a fraction, round down to the nearest whole number.

2. Lay the mottled metallic paper flat on a cutting mat. Using a straightedge and cutting blade, trim strips ¾" (2cm) wide. Cut strips in two lengths, one set long enough to wrap around the length of the box with a ¾" (2cm) overlap, the rest long enough to wrap around the width of the box with a ¾" (2cm) overlap.

3. Wrap the shorter strips around the width of the wrapped box, parallel to one another, with ¾" (2cm) of space between each strip. Dab glue on the strips at the box edges. Do not use glue on any other areas of the strips, because you will be weaving the perpendicular strips through. a

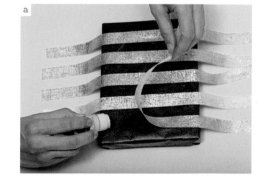

**4.** Create the woven pattern by positioning the longer strips perpendicular to the first set of strips. Weave each long strip under and over the shorter strips you've already placed on the box. Once each strip is in place, apply a dab of glue to the underside of each end to adhere them to the box's surface. b

**5.** Carefully turn the box over.

**6.** Use glue to close up what now resembles a band of paper. Remember to mimic the woven effect on the back side of the box, the same as what was executed on the front side, weaving the longer strips among the shorter strips. c

**7.** Turn the box over again, adjusting the placement of any strips as necessary. Place the berry gift topper on the top of the package and wrap the skinny gold twine around the top and the bottom of the stem multiple times to secure the topper to the box. d

WAX SEALS

Wax seals always say both "royalty" and "romance" to me, evoking a time when the pace of life was slower and people conducted their days with a sense of reverence and grace. In their heyday, wax seals added a sense of permanence and importance to the occasion, and they can impart these same feelings to your gift-giving today.

The silk-covered box shown here needed only an elegant closure, perfect for wax sealing. You can wrap your gift with any favorite fabric using the Basic Box Wrap (page 26) and a hot-glue gun, or you can use a decorative box.

## MATERIALS

small amount of oil (baby or olive oil is fine)

small cloth remnant or paper towel

3" (7.5cm) wide silk ribbon

silk-covered box or balsa wood box

match

wax burner with denatured alcohol

wax stick

decorative wax sealer

scissors

1. Prepare a cloth remnant or paper towel by pouring a very small amount of oil on it. Prior to stamping the sealer into the hot wax, you will stamp the sealer on the surface of this oiled piece. An oiled sealer will be less likely to stick to the warmed wax.

2. Bring the wide silk ribbon around the width of the box and up to the top of the box, tying it off with only a half-knot. a

3. Take both ribbon ends and hold them firmly together on the surface of the box.

You could also use a heavy, flat stone to anchor and hold the ribbon ends in place on the box's surface as the wax burner is prepared.

4. Light the wax burner. You may want to do this step before you wrap the ribbon around the box if you find that having two hands free is more comfortable.

5. Place the tip of the wax stick directly at the top of the flame to soften the wax tip. b

*Personalize* the gift even further by using a metal family monogram or crest ring instead of a traditional wax sealer. Just be sure that the ring has a generally flat surface so you can apply pressure evenly.

6. When the softened wax begins to pool—but before it drips onto the flame—move the softened tip of the wax stick away from the flame and place it directly onto the ribbon ends. Rotate the wax stick, leaving a puddle of wax on top of the ribbon ends. c

7. Repeat this step 6 to 8 times. The goal is to accumulate a puddle of wax large enough to accommodate the size of the wax seal.

NOTE: If random wax drippings happen to land on the box's surface, leave them there—they are a beautiful, accidental sign of the human hand!

8. Graze the wax sealer over the oiled cloth and then gently push the metal wax sealer into the warm wax puddle. Hold for approximately 6 to 10 seconds, or until the wax has hardened. d

9. Lift the sealer and admire your creation, and trim the ribbon ends to the desired length.

# NOSTALGIC GLINT

Romance can take different forms. Some people prefer high-impact shine, while others may yearn for a subtle, quiet glint. Here, the addition of fine glitter to the wrapping paper creates a refined aesthetic with muted shine. It is better to use papers with a matte finish, rather than ones with a high-gloss finish, because the glitter will better affix to paper with more "tooth."

To further achieve a romantic, nostalgic sensibility, I have used tea-stained flowers to embellish the gifts. One flower is made from cheesecloth (shown at left) and can be easily created at home by following the steps below. The other is a cotton flower gift topper.

1. Lay the paper on a flat surface. You may choose to glitter the entire sheet, perhaps having some paper left over for another gift wrap. Or you may want to glitter only the amount of paper needed for the particular gift you are about to wrap. If you choose the latter, determine how much paper you will need (page 24) before the glittering process.

2. Dip the string into the glue mixture, using both hands to hold the two ends and keeping your fingers and the ends of the string out of the glue bath. a

3. Softly shake off any excess glue over the glue-filled container to avoid unwanted drips. Delicately apply glue to the paper by pressing and lifting the string, following the striped pattern or, if you are working with a plain paper, appling the glue in a pattern of your choice. It will be necessary to dip the string in glue again as you work. b

   **NOTE:** Experiment with different lengths of string to achieve various patterns.

4. Once the glue application is complete, apply glitter directly to the glued areas by pinching glitter between your thumb and pointer finger and sprinkling it over the glue areas. c

5. Shake any excess glitter into an empty container for reuse.

## MATERIALS

striped or patterned lightweight paper

cotton string

all-purpose glue mixture, three parts glue to one part water, in a long, shallow container

gold glitter

silk ribbon, ¾" (2cm) width

narrow silk ribbon, ⅛" (3mm) width

tea-stained cheese-cloth remnant (Gauze Deconstructed, page 98)

tape

scissors

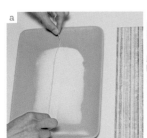

6. Allow the glue to dry, and wrap the gift using the paper and the Basic Box Wrap technique (page 26). Add the ribbons using the Layered Ribbon Tie technique (page 33), crossing the ribbons to one side of the box and finishing with a square knot.

7. To create the flower topper, use a tea-stained cheesecloth remnant measuring approximately 5" (12.5cm) wide by 18" (45.5cm) long. For instruction on tea-staining, refer to Gauze Deconstructed (page 98).

8. Roll the piece of cloth along its long length. When you reach the end, tie the roll securely with a piece of narrow ribbon or twine toward one end of the cloth "bundle." d

9. Trim the roll below the tie and mount the flower onto the gift, using the excess narrow silk ribbon tails to tie it onto the ribbon intersection of your wrapped package. e

**TIP** *Dusty pinks and reds, golden browns, and natural whites perfectly complement the demure tea-stained flowers and inspire wistful memories. The bit of glittered sparkle enlivens the pale, faded colors and keeps this package looking modern.*

**BLACK TIE BOX**

*Although the look of gold or silver is easy to emulate using the techniques from Nostalgic Glint, premade metallic papers are great gift wrap alternatives when you want to add some shine to a special package without mixing glue and glitter.*

*The Metallic Fusing paper, shown above in this simple yet stunning wrap, evokes both formality and fashion. It is a paper marvelous enough to exist on its own as home decor, but used here, the stark contrast of a rich black cord creates a dramatic presentation fitting for an elegant environment. Follow the steps for the Del Rosario Tie (page 36) to achieve this unusual ribbon tie.*

# BOTTLE WRAP

Imagine that someone special has invited you to a party. You bring over a bottle of wine, one of your favorites, and one that you would like to enjoy with your friends. But often the host is too busy to notice this carefully chosen bottle, and it is placed amid the myriad other bottles brought by other guests. Avoid this common problem by dressing up the bottle for the occasion. A special wrap will convey the stature of the gift and help it stand apart from bottles presented in ubiquitous premade wine bags. Of course, you can use this wrap for any bottled gift.

1. If you are using a paper that is slightly transparent, as shown, use tissue paper to create an opaque layer. Measure and cut both sheets of paper to the same size. The width of the papers should cover the circumference of the bottle plus an additional 2" (5cm). The length of the papers should measure the height of the bottle plus an additional 3"–4" (7.5cm–10cm).

2. Lay the tissue on top of the decorative sheet against its wrong side. Fold in and crease approximately 1" (2.5cm) along the top width of the papers, as well as one side length of the papers. These will become the clean folded-in edges appearing at the top of the bottle and along its side. Use double-side tape along the inside fold between the tissue paper and the decorative paper to keep the papers together as you wrap. a

3. Place the bottle on the paper with its length parallel and close to the long uncreased side of the paper, allowing approximately 2"–3" (5cm–7.5cm) of paper at the base. The top of the bottle should be nearest the folded edge of the paper.

4. Bring up the uncreased side of paper and, keeping the paper taut against the bottle, roll the bottle until you reach the end of the paper. Tape to secure. b

5. To finish the bottom of the bottle, fold in the ends of the paper on the bottom of the bottle using the pleating steps in the Cylinder Wrap technique (page 29)

6. Using one hand, gather the paper taut against the neck of the bottle, and secure with the Cotton Ball trim (page 126). c

**MATERIALS**

decorative paper

tissue paper

tape

large sewing needle

metallic twine

cotton balls

scissors

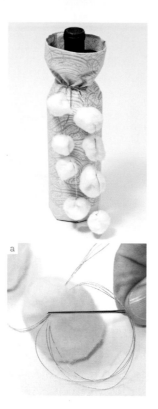

## COTTON BALL TRIM

1. Using the sewing needle threaded with four strands of gold metallic thread measuring 36" (91cm) each, thread four cotton balls each on both ends of the strands.

2. To secure each cotton ball in place, pull the needle through twice, the second time threading the needle through the metallic thread loop resulting from the second needle pass. a

NOTE: There is absolutely a playfulness to cotton balls, and when combined with a more elegant paper, the personality of the gift shines through. Of course, any pom-pom will do.

## WRAPPING OUTSIDE THE BOX

Wrapping odd-size gifts can be a creative challenge. However, don't be intimidated. Instead, ramp up your creative savvy and put it to work! Because each gift is unique, I couldn't begin to tell you how to wrap each oddly sized gift.

Keep in mind that gifts, especially large items, do not necessarily have to be wrapped entirely in paper to be given as a gift. If you are gifting a bicycle, for example, consider using colorful wide ribbons to weave in, out, and around the bicycle spokes. For tall objects, consider draping over the object three to four lengths (depending on size) of basic and economical brown kraft paper. Just allow the lengths to graze the floor and then cinch the paper lengths around the base with a wide wire-edged ribbon. If you can simply remember that the goal is not only to conceal the gift but also to enhance it, you will be able to cleverly create your own unique gift wraps for any occasion.

To me, decorating a gift is like accessorizing with jewelry. One must maintain the overall balance of the look while adding those "perfect touches" that make us feel special. Like pieces of jewelry one may wear for a special occasion, these crystals are strung in a planned yet random-looking fashion and appear to "float" on the gift. They highlight the presentation while adding a melodic grace to the stack of beautiful packages shown here.

## MATERIALS

magenta lokta paper

Japanese yuzen paper

double-side tape

gold crimped wire

clear crystal beads

scissors

1. Wrap the boxes with your chosen papers, keeping in mind the final desired order of the stack. Stack the three boxes, using a piece of double-side tape between each box to hold them in place if desired.

2. Measure out a length of wire that is long enough to go around the sides of the largest box, adding a 4" (10cm) excess. Thread 3 crystals in the middle of this wire, allowing approximately 1" (2.5cm) between each crystal. A simple twist of the wire around each crystal keeps it securely positioned.

3. Wrap the sides of this box with the beaded crimped wire, twisting the ends together at the back. Finish the ends by molding the wire with your fingers into a tiny wire rosette. a Make sure that the three crystals are positioned in the middle of the box front. b

4. Measure out 2 pieces of wire that are long enough to wrap around the stack of all three boxes, each with a 4" (10cm) excess. These pieces will wrap parallel to each other and perpendicular to the first wire strand. Thread 4 sets of 3 crystals on each of these wires, being aware of your desired final placement of the crystals on the box stack.

5. Wrap the first wire strand around the box stack, positioning the wire ends to finish off to the side of the bottom box.

6. Wrap the second wire around the box stack about 3" (7.5cm) apart from the wire that you just placed, positioning its wire ends to finish off on the same side of the bottom box.

7. Cut a 6" (15cm) piece of wire and string it with one crystal, positioning it at the wire's midpoint. Pinch the two long wire strands together at the top of the gift and twist the 6" (15cm) piece around them to secure. For the finishing touch, curl the wire ends to create tiny rosettes. c

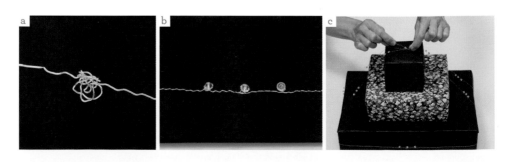

As you choose the papers in which to wrap your special packages, be bold when combining colors and patterns. But balance a rich combination with a simple embellishment, keeping in mind design principle 02. Emphasize Simplicity (page 10).

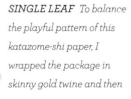

**SINGLE LEAF** *To balance the playful pattern of this katazome-shi paper, I wrapped the package in skinny gold twine and then used that same twine around the stem of the leaf topper itself. Finally, I wrapped the twine around both the leaf and the package. The band of crushed velvet separates the leaf from the patterned paper, allowing it to "pop" off the background.*

# STRING OF FLOWERS

I love combing flea markets, craft shops, and hobby shops for little things that catch my eye. These charming little flowers were found at a party supply shop, and when they were brought into Soolip, everybody was so anxious to use them. The adults were just as attracted to these little gems as were the children. Creating a gift like this one is like creating a playful collage. Try to keep in mind who the gift is going to, and choose trinkets that you think your friend will love.

## MATERIALS

glitter paper, or other decorative paper

clear plastic flowers, or alternative adornment

crimped wire

white all-purpose glue and paintbrush, or hot-glue gun

tape

scissors

1. Wrap the package with glitter paper using the Basic Box Wrap method (page 26).

2. Wrap crimped wire around the box 4 times, making sure the wire strands are spaced out to accommodate the width of the flower adornments.

3. Use a brush to apply glue to the backs of the plastic flowers, and place them on top of the wire. Press firmly to secure. a, b

*The Soolip Fix*    *Beauty is everywhere around us, and many times in the most unexpected places.*

Just because an object lacks inherent function doesn't mean you have to throw it away. Sock away those broken necklaces or buttons and consider your stash as design elements to be used in gift wrapping. Finding just the right use for them is not only fun but also resourceful!

# RIBBON-WRAPPED CYLINDER

Often, the presents we give fit nicely within the four walls of a square or rectangular box, whether that box be flat, tall, thick, or squat. But there are some packages that will require a cylindrical wrap.

Adding quiet luxury to this wrap are the yards of skinny silk ribbon girding this package in a beautiful way. When it is completed, this ribbon tie seems breathtakingly impossible, but don't be discouraged from mastering the technique, as it follows basic ribbon-tie methods. Nestled beneath the ribbon are neat tucks of paper at each end of the cylinder, crisp reminders of the beauty in simplicity.

## MATERIALS

Japanese yuzen paper, or a lightweight paper

skinny silk ribbon

tweezers

tape

scissors

1. Use the yuzen paper to wrap the package, following the instructions for the Cylinder Wrap (page 29).

2. To embellish the cylinder with ribbon, use a variation of the Multi-Wrap Ribbon Tie (page 34). Begin with one end of the ribbon held in place with one hand. Refrain from trimming the ribbon off its spool until you have completed wrapping the ribbon around the cylinder. **a**

3. Using the other hand, wrap the long length of the ribbon around the cylinder eight times, each time passing at the top in the middle and keeping the ribbon secure at the center with your other hand. You can wrap the ribbon around the cylinder fewer times, if desired. **b**

4. When you finish wrapping the ribbon, trim the end from the spool with scissors, leaving an excess of 10" (25.5cm) for the bow and the tails.

5. Use tweezers to thread one ribbon end under and through the crossing point of the ribbon, forming a loop around that intersection. **c**

6. Tie the bow and trim the tails to the desired length. **d**

# DRIPPING AMARANTHUS

Adding fresh foliage to a gift is often unexpected, but it complements a gift with poise. Romantic amaranthus stems cascading over the multiple levels of sumptuously wrapped boxes make this perfect for a wedding or anniversary gift wrap. Blossoming floral vines, such as jasmine or passion fruit, are also ideal for this project. Unless you will be giving this gift immediately after you wrap it, it's best to place water tubes (available at most florists) at the ends of the stems to maintain the longevity of these live cuttings. Or you may wish to affix the fresh foliage to the prewrapped gift upon your arrival at the event.

1. Wrap boxes, each different in size, with the decorative papers using the Basic Box Wrap (page 26). It is ideal that the box on top have a taller, more vertical, shape than the box that it sits on, which will allow enough space for the amaranthus to fall down the stack.

2. Tie all three colors of silk ribbon around the stacked boxes using the Multi-Wrap Ribbon Tie (page 34).

3. To create the floral gift topper, trim the leaves off the base of the amaranthus stems up to 4" (10cm) with the floral scissors. If you are using water tubes, trim the stems up to 7" (18cm) to ensure that you have enough stem to accommodate the water tubes and to wrap the ribbons around.

4. Group the three stems using floral tape, wrapping the area where the leaves were trimmed.

5. Place one end of the natural silk ribbon parallel to the stems, allowing 8"–12" (20.5cm–30.5cm) of excess beyond the end of the stems for the streamers. Begin wrapping the stems, following the bundling technique instructions from Bundle of Twigs (page 54). a, b

6. Wrap the chocolate and the pink ribbons in a crisscross pattern over the natural silk handle, finishing at the bottom and leaving an 8"–12" (20.5cm–30.5cm) tail for the streamers. c

7. Attach this floral piece to the top of the boxes, using 12" (30.5cm) ribbon strands, thereby creating a voluptuous collection of silk strands falling over the boxes. Allow the floral piece to cascade over the top box and down the sides of the stack of gifts. d

## MATERIALS

decorative papers

½" (13mm) natural silk ribbon

⅜" (9mm) wide chocolate and pale-pink silk ribbons

3 stems of amaranthus or blossoming floral vines

floral scissors to trim foliage

water tubes, if needed

floral tape

tape

scissors

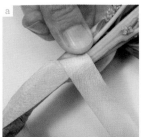

# PAPER LACE AND FLOWERS

A sumptuous flower bouquet gift topper is always a delight to receive, as it transitions from gift to vase with ease. The delicate paper-thin petals and perfect pink hue of these peonies set the stage for a romantic and endearing occasion.

To heighten the feeling of romance, I have used elements from a very special washi lace paper. There are many Japanese lace papers readily available in paper and art stores. Though delicate in appearance, these lace papers are resistant to tears, creases, and folds, because the kozo plant fibers that make up the paper are left long to strengthen the finished paper.

## MATERIALS

lightweight to medium-weight solid-color paper

paper lace

crushed-velvet ribbon, 1" (2.5cm) width

two fresh peonies or other cut flowers

water tubes (optional)

white all-purpose glue and small paint-brush (optional), for glue application

scissors

1. Separate and clean the flower stems of excess stem or wilted greenery. Trim the stems at an angle with scissors, as this will help to preserve the blooms.

2. Wrap your box in the solid paper. I used a wine-colored lokta paper.

3. Determine how much of the box you want the lace to accent. It can be a simple narrow band of paper lace, or you may decide to cover all of the box. Whatever you choose, be certain that you cut a length long enough to wrap completely around the box. a

4. Apply small dots of glue to the underside of the paper lace piece. Carefully place the lace band on one surface of the box and wrap the lace band around the box until it meets itself, softly patting it with your hand to assist in adhering the lace band to the box. b

5. Wrap the crushed-velvet ribbon around the box using the Flat-Base Ribbon Tie method (page 32). Before you tie a full knot, place the two peonies with trimmed 5"–6" (12.5cm–15cm) stems at the ribbon's intersection. Then complete the knot, securing the peonies to the package. c

*Like most fresh flowers, peonies stay fresh for about three to four hours without water in temperate climates. To extend the life of your flowers, use water tubes at the ends of their stems.*

# Living life with beauty and inspiration

*At Soolip there is a consciousness in all that we do when we create, and a joy when we share our creations with others. For me, there is nothing more beautiful and moving than what is made by the human hand and the heart. When I give of my time, energy, and creativity to others, I am not just giving a present, I am giving myself. This passion for reaching out and connecting with my friends and family has led me through the pages of this book and, I hope, guides you as you embark on your own journey through art and craft. Whether using materials found in a boutique paper emporium, a local sewing store, a five-and-dime, or even your own backyard, unleash your creative spirit and seek what speaks to your heart. With the right tools, techniques, and materials, you will truly discover the art of gift wrapping.*

*Most important, have fun and be inspired!*

*With love,*

# ACKNOWLEDGMENTS

Heartfelt thanks go to all who have contributed to my journey of creating my first book:

To my photographer, Jules Bianchi, for her amazing ability to capture what I see in my heart.

To my colleague and styling partner Vanessa Tamayo, for being an inspiration to me every day and for always being unafraid to move us into new territory.

To my editor Rebecca Behan for dedicating herself to the perfection of my work, and for making this book gracefully flow.

To my art director, Chi Ling Moy, and graphic designer, La Tricia Watford, for executing a perfect marriage of all the book's elements into a single, stunning vision.

To my agent, Peter McGuigan of Foundry Media, whose guidance in the world of book publishing has made creating this book such a positive experience.

To Laura Tremaine, Jennifer Barguiarena, Amy Schadt, and Ann Marie Boyle for their spirited energy and their experienced styling.

To the generous paper and ribbon suppliers, my friends who have given me guidance and support for so many years: Manohar Devraj at Xylem, Michael Ginsberg at Legion Paper, Pierre Guidan at Savoir Faire, Manish Gupta at Handmade Expressions, Lynn Mitchell, as well as those at Hanah Silk, Midori Ribbon, and Studio Athena.

To the Soolip family: Cruz Arreotua, Katherine Clark, Ana Lugo, Nicol Raglan, Delfina Ramirez, Maria Ramirez, Aleksey Shirikov, Susan Silvestri, Vanessa Tamayo, Ashley Tearston, Florentino Vargas—as well as Soolip friends Constantine del Rosario, Karla Duran, Kristen Gava, Billy Hutchinson, Sharon Lowe, Timothy Pogoler, and Gloria Shen.

To my dear friends for their years of unending support and friendship: Adrianna de la Parre, Tom Hoffman, Elizabeth Hubbell, Brenda Smith, Richard Smith, Karen Tangorra, Catherine Wimberg, and Barbara Wolf.

To my love, George Burke, who has brought so much into my life.

To my mom and dad, my brother, William Wen, and my sister, Wendy Wen, who all have supported me in so many ways.

To my children, Simone, Dag (thanks for the origami birds!), and Odin. You are my true teachers and inspiration. I love you all so much.

I dedicate this book to the late Grant Edwin Forsberg, my husband and ex-husband, father to my children, business partner, and friend. You believed in me . . . and still do.

## ABOUT THE AUTHOR

WANDA WEN is the founder and creative force behind Soolip, the Los Angeles paper and lifestyle boutique that is a favorite among Hollywood celebrities, tastemakers, and corporate clients. Wen has successfully combined her passions for paper and nature with her background in fashion, launching the unique brand Soolip with multiple extensions and satellite businesses.

Wen and Soolip have been featured in numerous publications, including *Martha Stewart Weddings*, *Town & Country*, *Vogue*, *InStyle*, *Elegant Bride*, *Travel + Leisure*, *People*, *The New York Times*, and *The Wall Street Journal*. Wen has also appeared on *Today*, *HGTV*, the Style Network, E!, and the Fine Living Channel. She is also an expert gift wrapper for Scotch brand and a judge for the annual Scotch Brand Most Gifted Wrapper Contest.

Wen resides in Los Angeles with her three children, a dog, two birds, and a guinea pig. Visit her online at www.soolip.com, asoolipwedding.com, and www.soolip.blogspot.com.

## ABOUT THE PHOTOGRAPHER

JULES BIANCHI received a camera from her father at age twelve and has been capturing moments frozen in time ever since. Today she works in wedding, family, pet, and lifestyle photography and is an active speaker on wedding photography, inspiration, and technique. Her photographs have been published in magazines such as *The Knot*, *Your Wedding Day*, and *Los Angeles Weddings*. Bianchi lives in West Hollywood, California, with her fluffy dog, Olive.

Visit her online at www.julesbianchi.com.

## RESOURCE GUIDE

Most of the ingredients used in this book, from nature's findings to vintage beads and handmade papers, are things we use in our gift-wrap service at Soolip every day. We'd love to see you at the store or have you visit us online.

SOOLIP

8646 Melrose Avenue
West Hollywood,
California 90069

310.360.0545
www.soolip.com

When hunting for trims and findings, take a trip to a yarn or sewing store for a wide selection of notions. A bead store also should have a myriad of findings from which to choose the perfect accents for your package. When you shop, don't worry about duplicating exactly what you see in this book. Visit your favorite shops and go with what catches your eye. Choosing new and unexpected elements for gift wrap is part of the fun.

### ART SUPPLIES

Dick Blick
www.dickblick.com
*decorative paper, paintbrushes, gold leaf*

Michael's
www.michaels.com
*paintbrushes, gold leaf, yarn*

Jo-Ann Fabrics and Crafts
www.joann.com
*sewing supplies, floral tape, fabric, embroidery thread, gold and silver thread*

Silvercrow Creations
www.silvercrowcreations.com
*mica flakes*

### BEADS

Harlequin Beads
1027 Willamette Street
Eugene, Oregon 97401
www. harlequinbeads.com
*beads, Swarovski crystals*

Sweets Beads
7763½ Beverly Boulevard
Los Angeles, California 90036
www.sweetsbeads.com
*notions, beads, Swarovski crystals*

### FLOWERS & FOLIAGE

Armstrong Garden
www.armstronggarden.com
*plants, herbs, twigs, river stones*

Floracopia at Soolip
8646 Melrose Avenue
West Hollywood, California 90069
310.659.9537

Pressed Flower Gallery
www.pressedflower.com
*pressed flowers, leaves*

Sego Nursery
12126 Burbank Boulevard
Valley Village, California 91607
818.763.5711
*plants, herbs, twigs*

Sheridan Gardens
817 N. Hollywood Way
Burbank, California 91505
www.sheridangardens.com

## JAPANESE DECORATIVE PAPER

Hiromi Paper International
2525 Michigan Avenue
Santa Monica, California 90404
www.hiromipaper.com

Kiteya Soho
464 Broome Street
New York, New York 10013
www.kiteyany.com
*paper, Japanese wrapping cloth, obi ribbon*

Miki's Paper
1801 4th Street
Berkeley, California 94710
510.845.9530

The Paper Place
887 Queen Street West
Toronto Ontario M6J 1G5
Canada
www.thepaperplace.ca

## KITCHEN SUPPLIES & SUNDRIES

Sur La Table
www.surlatable.com
*cheesecloth*

Walgreens
www.walgreens.com
*waxed paper, crayons, glue, shoelaces,
peppermint candies*

## OFFICE SUPPLIES

Staples
www.staples.com
*kraft paper, manila tags, crayons, glue,
pencils, double-side tape, scissors, cotton
string*

## RIBBON, TWINE, & GIFT TOPPERS

Bell'occhio
10 Brady Street
San Francisco, California 94103
www.bellocchio.com

Tinsel Trading Company
1 West 37th Street
New York, New York 10018
www.tinseltrading.com

The Caning Company
926 Gilman Street
Berkeley, California 94710
www.caningshop.com
*waxed twine*

## PAPER & STATIONERY BOUTIQUES

Black Ink
101 Charles Street
Boston, Massachusetts 02114
www.blackinkboston.com

Broadway Paper
191 North Broadway
Milwaukee, Wisconsin 53202
www.broadwaypaper.com

De Medici Ming Fine Paper
1222 1st Avenue, Ste. A
Seattle, Washington 98101
206.624.1983

Greer
1657 North Wells Street
Chicago, Illinois 60614
312.337.8000
www.greerchicago.com

Just Paper and Tea
3232 P Street Northwest
Washington D.C. 20007
www.justpaperandtea.com

Kate's Paperie
Multiple locations in
New York City and
surrounding areas
www.katespaperie.com

Oblation
516 NW 12th Avenue
Portland, Oregon 97209
www.oblationpapers.com

On Paper
737 North High Street
Columbus, Ohio 43215
www.onpaper.com

Paper Connection
166 Doyle Avenue
Providence, Rhode Island 02906
www.paperconnection.com

Paper Source
Locations nationwide
www.paper-source.com

Scriptura
5423 Magazine Street
New Orleans, Louisiana 70115
www.scriptura.com

Two Hands Paperie
803 Pearl Street
Boulder, Colorado 80302
www.twohandspaperie.com

----

MY FAVORITE
INSPIRATION
STORES

Cursive New York
ABC Carpet and Home
888 Broadway
New York, New York 10003
www.cursivenewyork.com

De Vera
1 Crosby Street
New York, New York 10013

29 Maiden Lane
San Francisco, California
94108
www.deveraobjects.com

Meg Cohen Design Shop
59 Thompson Street
New York, New York 10012
212.966.3733
www.megcohendesign.com

The Gardener
1836 Fourth Street
Berkeley, California 94710
www.thegardener.com

----

# INDEX